The Powerful Percent

Students at the Heart of the Great Commission

The Powerful Percent

Students at the Heart of the Great Commission

Patricia Burgin

WSN
PRESS

Worldwide Student NetWork Press

SALEM EVANGELICAL FREE CHURCH

The Powerful Percent
©1991, Patricia Burgin
All rights reserved
Printed in the United States of America

Published by
Worldwide Student NetWork Press
100 Sunport Lane
Orlando, FL 32809

Library of Congress Cataloging-in-Publication Data
(pending)

ISBN 0-9629245-0-4

Unless otherwise indicated, Scripture quotations
are from *The New International Version* (NIV) ©1985
by The Zondervan Corporation.

For clarity, pronouns referring to God, Jesus Christ
and/or the Holy Spirit are capitalized except where
directly quoted without capitalization.

This book is for and about you: the world's powerful percent, as you discover for yourself the joy of following Jesus Christ in this, your moment in history.

Contents

Acknowledgments

Digging into the writing of a first book is a great time to be reminded that a lot of the best things you know, you've learned from the people who have known you the longest. I'm grateful for the affirmation and grace of my family, beginning, of course, with my parents, Glen and Georgia, who are constant and extravagant givers of confidence.

Since the summer of 1972, a team of financial backers has underwritten my ministry, and in so doing, has helped to give rise to this book and to a small part of the worldwide movement it reflects. These people have taught me tenacity and generosity.

I'm grateful to Susan Westlake Hutcheson for her friendship and for her encouragement to so many, especially to me, to learn from our spiritual forebears. Many of Susan's conclusions are happily incorporated into chapter two.

My most personal lessons about the global nature of the gospel have come on cold Russian nights over cups of steaming black tea. I'm thankful for Anatole and Irina, Natasha, Helena and Sergei, for Valery and Andrei, Olga and Sasha, Tamara and Vladilen. They are wise and patient friends.

Thanks to Jay and Olgy Gary. Their loyal friendship and wise counsel have followed me since we first met in Edinburgh a decade ago. They are now emerging as two of the finest young missiologists of this generation. Their determination to understand the flow and the lessons of history are reflected in chapter two. Their clear view of our present progress and future possibilities in reaching and mobilizing students of the world helped to sharpen chapter four.

Thanks to some longtime kindred spirits who have walked with Christ, loved students and encouraged me: the members, past and present, of the Campus Ministry National Team of Campus Crusade for Christ. I am especially grateful to Bill and Vonette Bright as they mark forty years of faithfulness to the idea that has captured us all.

And thanks especially to Nancy Cahill, Terry and Carolyn Culbertson, Mary Graham, Cindy Harsh, Susan Westlake Hutcheson, Tina Jacobs, Debbie Jones, Sylvia Lindgren, John and Kari Medina, Martha Norberg, Roger and Sara Randall, Jayne Ross, Denny and Marilyn Rydberg, and Mary Walker who steadily remind me that I am not alone.

In all ages, the great creative religious ideas have been the achievement of the intellectual and spiritual insight of [young men and women] . . . many of the most revolutionary ideas have been worked out by [young people] under thirty and frequently by youths between eighteen and twenty-five.[1]

C. P. Shedd
Historian of the
Student Volunteer Movement

Society in this country owes its thanks to [students]. It was they who pushed history again. After twenty years, the students have returned history and time to this country.

Vaclav Havel
President of Czechoslovakia
USA Today, 11/27/89

This is a morning on which you can almost feel the world changing.

Charles Kuralt
CBS News, 6/4/89

< 1 >

The One-Percent Factor

While the world watched, hundreds of thousands of Chinese students and sympathizers filled Beijing's Tiananmen Square. For seven weeks they staged a non-violent protest. Erecting a huge white statue called the "Goddess of Democracy" to symbolize their cause, they demanded greater freedom and democracy from the Chinese government and called for an end to tyranny and corruption.

Before dawn on June 4, 1989, People's Liberation Army troops stormed the unarmed protestors, smashing frail barricades, and rolling tanks into the square. Soldiers raked the crowd with bullets, and the protestors fled as one. Pandemonium spread as people fell and vehicles burned. By morning, the troops had finished, the statue lay in ruins, and five hundred to a thousand supporters of the democracy movement were dead. The courageous actions of the young protestors and the ensuing bloodbath sent shock waves around the world.

Once again, students were on the cutting edge of change.

In this final decade of the second millennium, students make up about 1 percent of the world's population. Between fifty and sixty million men and women, mostly young, now attend colleges and universities around the world. All but about twelve million study outside of North America. Many already speak English as a second or third language.

As these young people were growing up, the Cold War ended, the planet's environment worsened. Responding to the physical emergencies of millions of people caught in the paths of typhoons and tyrants, the nations of the world began a new level of cooperation and communication. The generation that will inherit this scenario will be led by university graduates. Soon these men and women will lead governments, media, education, business, religion and the worldwide Christian movement into the 21st century. These students are the "powerful percent."

Let's step back twenty years to get a good vantage point on some of the realities that have shaped the powerful percent.

An Eruption of Student Power

The number of students enrolled in American colleges and universities doubled between 1963 and 1973. That giant wave was one of history's turning points: The baby-boom generation had grown up. Donald Shockley writes:

> From the time they were born until they went to college, the children of the baby boom were socialized in such fashion as to create a generation characterized by extraordinarily high expectations. Almost everything they encountered was new and apparently created for their benefit—houses, cars, schools, churches, shopping malls, toys, and television. It was an energetic, expanding, prosperous, benevolent world, and they seemed to be the center of its interest and concern. They were brought up in an environment in which their needs were critically important, and they had every reason to believe that they could control their own future. When they got to college, however, the conditions of life in the world seemed suddenly to be

turning against them and, to put it mildly, they were not pleased.[2]

In the late 1960s, I was one of those exuberant boomers. I began my freshman year in college in the fall of 1968. Everywhere I looked, tragedy took us by surprise.

That year began with a terrible defeat. America started losing her way in Vietnam. By spring, 525,000 troops were on the battlefields. More than 100,000 Americans, mostly men who could have been my classmates, had been wounded or killed in military action.

On April 4, Dr. Martin Luther King Jr., leader of the civil rights movement, was assassinated in Memphis. On April 27, there were massive student demonstrations against the war. At the same time, a movie about a "Graduate" losing his idealism and innocence played in theaters across the country.

On June 4, Bobby Kennedy was shot to death moments after his victory speech in the California Democratic presidential primary.

Through the summer, the poor marched in Washington, and people starved to death in an African country none of us had ever heard of. In August, headlines told of the brutal Soviet invasion of Czechoslovakia and of massive rioting in the streets of Chicago during the Democratic National Convention. In November, Richard Nixon was elected president, and the Beatles were beginning to fade out, singing songs of resignation. At Christmas, Apollo 8 circled the moon, taking three astronauts into the profound radio silence on the far side.

During that wild year, religion was not a chief concern. My classmates and I thought of ourselves as moderately and appropriately religious. For us, religion was a nostalgic attachment to church, celebrating with the family at Christmas and Easter, and maintaining fairly moral behavior in between. It had never occurred to us that anything of a radical or revolutionary nature could ever be associated with God. Religion was a comfortable presence, as long as it stayed in its place.

The events of the day led us to develop passionate convictions. But holding to moral absolutes about things like God or our sexuality, we reasoned, only led to intolerance—the only absolutely wrong thing we could think of.

By the fall of 1970, those passionate convictions were fading. Despite our numbers and our power, the world wasn't changing. Worse, I wasn't changing into the kind of person I really wanted to be. I had, as we used to say, the "blahs about the cause." Besides, after seeing the "free-speech movement" from the inside, I was unsettled with the hypocrisy and moral tourism that marked much of what went on. I had listened to talk about freedom without boundaries, but the people who talked the loudest weren't known for their personal peace or for the quality of their relationships.

Perhaps the most well-known part of the Bible to many of us was King Solomon's journal, the Book of Ecclesiastes. A rock group even put Solomon's lyrics in chapter three to music. He thought about birth and death and planting and killing and weeping and laughing and embracing and searching and quietness and healing and love and war and peace. So did we. We thought a lot about vanity. So did he.

On a cold October afternoon in 1970, as I was leafing through those pages, I noticed Solomon's observation that life would be far easier had God not planted "eternity in our hearts." Solomon wrote:

> [God] has made everything beautiful in its time. He has also set eternity in the hearts of men; yet they cannot fathom what God has done from beginning to end (Ecclesiastes 3:11).

This king, my fellow pilgrim, seemed to be saying, *Look. If you are serious about wanting to understand the issues of life, you must relate intimately with the One who says He made you, who says He loves you, and who says He wants you to know Him personally. The One whose truth gives form and power to freedom. Without Him, all of life is vanity.*

As I read the words, I considered the possibility that they were true, that I was not here by chance, but by choice. If I was here by God's choice, maybe I could have a relationship with Him. On that day, I paused and quietly asked Jesus Christ to begin to show me answers to my questions and doubts.

What Changes, What Doesn't

Some questions and issues will never change. *Eternity* will always be in our hearts, and students will always stay up late talking about vanity and birth and death and planting and killing and weeping and laughing and embracing and searching and quietness and healing and love and war and peace.

Something else that will never change is the way Jesus Christ can give wisdom to His followers to explain the gospel's relevance to those issues.

When the biggest groups on campus were fraternities and sororities, Christian students and Campus Crusade for Christ staff began speaking in their living rooms. When the free-speech movement had

its radical grip on the University of California at
Berkeley, they launched the "Christian World
Liberation Front." They began competitive athletic
teams and spawned Christian singing groups. And
when students began to spend spring break on the
beaches of Florida and California, so did they.

Today, students have grown up learning to listen
more to the needs and opinions of other nations.
American society has become more sensitive to racial
fairness.

Christian students are still making indelible
marks too, only now the marks are routinely global
and cross-cultural. Transportation and communication have expanded possibilities for more students
from more countries to follow Christ to all parts of
the world.

We can be grateful that some things never change.

Students continue to challenge things. A cultural
generation has passed, and the values of my generation of the boomers-turned-hippies-turned-yuppies-
turned-seekers are up for review.

True, there were 72 million of us born between
1946 and 1964. And since we began reaching adult-
hood in the late '60s, by sheer force of numbers, we
have tended to call the shots, reweaving the tapestry
of American values and causes and question marks.
Now we're getting competition from the not-so-quiet
new generation: the youngest of the "boomers," and
"the baby-busters," or what *Fortune Magazine*
recently dubbed, "yiffies: young, individualistic,
freedom-minded, and few." Few. That's the 48
million people who were between eighteen and
twenty-nine when the '90s began.

With the final decade of the millennium, this new
generation of students is arriving with a wonderful
challenge of its own. Students are insisting on emo-

tional balance and ethical steadiness. They will spend their time and money on adventure and experience instead of, like too many of their parents, on acquisitions. Vocationally, they will seek a good personal "fit." And they will seek to do all of the above in the context of committed relationships.

These will be the human architects of history in the 21st century.

"You Can Almost Feel the World Changing"

I used to wonder if I would recognize history in the making. From Eastern Europe to China to the Middle East, you "can almost feel the world changing." If you've read a paper, listened to the news, or better yet, gone to see for yourself, you know that Mr. Kuralt's words were true—and not just for that morning after the massacre of students on Tiananmen Square, and not just for China.

I'm beginning to think that these final years of the 1900s will go down in history with some of the hopes and passions and infamies of any great turning point in history. Nations that have been dominated by militant atheism for much of the 20th century are changing. The vacuum created by years of militant atheism or by an incomplete image of God has left behind social, emotional, economic and spiritual wreckage.

The vacuum, on the other hand, is also characterized by the sweet enthusiasm to freely consider the claims of Jesus Christ. Students and professors who have had virtually no background in biblical Christianity, are asking questions and responding to the love of Jesus Christ, particularly as they observe it in His followers. Personal and political openness as well as authentic Christianity are taking deep root in new believers.

And, as noted by observers like Vaclav Havel and Charles Kuralt, students are on the cutting edge of the changes. Architects, shaping the future.

There's always been something extraordinary about students. Throughout history they have been on the frontlines of revolutionary change. Their energy and idealism have fueled the gospel's advance through every generation. And just as university-aged people have carved deep marks of influence through the past 2,000 years, students today are on the verge of leaving their mark on the final years of this millennium. Their work, too, will be felt for all eternity.

These are all impressive, strategic reasons why students are uniquely qualified for helping to change the world. But in God's economy, the world changes one life at a time.

Following Aslan

At a dramatic point in C.S. Lewis' children's fantasy, *The Chronicles of Narnia,* the four children are being prepared to meet Aslan, a magnificent talking lion. As a Presence in the story, Aslan bears a striking resemblance to the Lion of Judah, Jesus Christ.

> *"Who is Aslan?" asked Susan.*
>
> *"Aslan?" said Mr. Beaver, "Why, don't you know? He's the King. He's the Lord of the whole world . . ."*
>
> *"Then he isn't safe?" said Lucy.*
>
> *"Safe?" said Mr. Beaver. "Don't you hear what Mrs. Beaver tells you? Who said anything about safe? Course he isn't safe. But he's good. He's the King, I tell you."*

Taking the gospel of Jesus Christ to the powerful percent has never been a safe proposition. But it's always been a good one.

For the majority of the world's 60 million university students, no one is there to tell them about Jesus Christ.

They are, in the words of Jesus, "lost"—sheep separated from the care and affection of the Shepherd.

Have you ever been lost? I mean really lost? Out of options and out of energy? Somewhere between puzzled and despondent? A usual feature of being lost is separation from an important relationship.

Jesus spoke of spiritual lostness with intensity. On one occasion He risked His reputation by reaching out to a wealthy chief tax collector in the town of Jericho. The man, known and avoided by the religious establishment as "a sinner," responded to Jesus' invitation. Significantly, as soon as a relationship was established between the man, Zacchaeus, and Jesus, Zacchaeus began to rebuild the trust that he had broken with the people around him.

"Jesus said to him, 'Today salvation has come to this house . . . For the Son of Man came to seek and to save what was lost'" (Luke 19:9,10).

In the mind of Jesus Christ, lostness meant the ultimate ruin of a personality. The men and women He encountered, like us, were designed to experience the well-being of a full, uncondemned and energizing relationship with a loving Creator.

People stay lost for a variety of reasons. Jesus discussed some of them in the three stories found in the fifteenth chapter of Luke's Gospel. As the chapter begins, Jesus speaks of a lost sheep—an animal which had wandered off because of ignorance or deception, and was then found through the diligence of the shepherd who rejoiced at the rescue.

Jesus then recounted the story of a woman who searched her home for a lost coin, the equivalent of a day's wage. The coin too was found after a diligent search. Then Luke observed that she, too, rejoiced.

Finally, Jesus relates the story of the lost son: a magnificent telling of the other elements of lostness—rebellion, sin, longing, humiliation, repentance and restoration. A defiant son becomes lost because of his own rebellion, and then, Jesus said, "He came to his senses." After rehearsing what he would say, the son returned to his father who was waiting expectantly and with compassion. The father also "had to celebrate and be glad, because [his son] was lost and is found."

In the stories, Jesus explained, being lost could result from ignorance, deception, or sheer defiance. The compassionate diligence of the search is the common thread weaving the parables together.

During the pre-glasnost days of fear and repression, a Soviet student listened to me present the gospel to individuals and groups over the course of a few days in Leningrad. She seemed to begin to understand. Pulling me aside, she said, "Patricia, you remind me of (she searched for the word) . . . 'missionary.'"

Of course I had been very careful to avoid being thought of as a traditional missionary during those days, so I looked nonchalant *(Who, me?)* and asked her to elaborate.

"Well," she continued, "many years ago we Russians were forced to forget about God. And we have been lost. Now you have come to help us to remember."

My young friend's lostness was a result of political and social forces as well as her spiritual condition. She needed me to come looking for her, to help her search out her dark corners, to show her that "God did not send his Son into the world to condemn the world, but to save the world through [Jesus Christ]" (John 3:17).

The more I travel the world, the more I become aware of the different expressions of what lostness looks like—and of the completeness of Christ's salvation. The results of lostness are evident intellectually and emotionally in relationships, and sometimes sin and deceit extend their effects even to the physical dimension of life.

But no matter what else accompanies life without Christ, being "lost" is always, and essentially, an issue of the soul. In his great wealth, King Solomon was able to say, "I denied myself nothing my eyes desired; I refused my heart no pleasure" (Ecclesiastes 2:10). But, even so, he felt lostness in his soul and ached in his mid-life emptiness.

Jesus recognized and responded to lostness. The eighth and ninth chapters of Matthew describe a very busy and very public time in His ministry. Over the course of a few days, He performed physical healings of leprosy, paralysis and fever. He dealt with people oppressed by demons, and challenged His disciples to deeper levels of commitment. Then there was another round of healing, more demons, Pharisees to be confronted, and even some public ridicule. As Jesus reaches the evening of one of these days, Matthew observed and then recorded:

> When he saw the crowds, he had compassion on them, because they were harassed and helpless, like sheep without a shepherd. Then

he said to his disciples, "The harvest is plentiful but the workers are few. Ask the Lord of the harvest, therefore, to send out workers into his harvest field" (Matthew 9:36-38).

In the great university centers of Europe and what has been the Soviet Union, in China and in the Middle East, throughout Africa, Latin America and North America, it's a new day: People are distressed and downcast; laborers are still few, but by the thousands, students are finding the Shepherd.

As we go, relating with people who don't yet know Christ, we've got to keep in mind a couple of powerful realities. The first is that same mercy Matthew saw reflected in the face of Jesus—compassion for the crowds because they were "like sheep without a shepherd."

But there is a second reality. Even without Christ, men and women still bear the image of God. Writer and philosopher Edith Schaeffer calls this quality, "leftover beauty." Christian students encounter this beauty in the face of ethnic and national uniqueness: the beauty and color and exuberance of people in the image of God who, when respectfully and personally approached, are eager to listen to new information about God's love and forgiveness in Jesus.

Part of our job is to remind each other of the companionship and power of the Good Shepherd Himself. Through former generations, He has shown His faithfulness to seek and to save and then to use students. And the ironclad precedent of His faithfulness to those who have gone before us is now ours to inherit.

The One-Percent Factor

In October of 1835, a young man entered Bonn University in Germany. Abandoning his Christian training, he became part of the "Young Hegelians" and spent many hours in long philosophical and political discussions. In 1844, at age twenty-six, he and another German intellectual, Friedrich Engels, embraced communism.

The student's name was Karl Marx, and the ideals he learned at the university and in his first job changed his life. He went on to co-author the *Communist Manifesto* and to become one of the most influential men in modern history. In the past decades, his theories have caused deprivation, disillusionment and death for millions of people in Europe, Asia and many so-called Third World countries.

Another young German studied law at Wittenberg University from 1716 to 1719. Years before, he had read a missionary paper and made a solemn promise that he would confess Christ and seek the conversion of men and women. He kept that vow and looked for ways to serve his Lord.

At twenty-two years of age, he allowed a group of persecuted Brethren families to settle on his estate. Soon this young man and his new friends organized themselves into a group known as the Moravians.

This young man's name was Count Nicholas von Zinzendorf. Although few in number, he looked upon the members of the Moravian Church as soldiers of Christ, able in love to conquer the world for their King. The Moravians—the first Protestant group to take seriously Christ's command to go into all the world with His message—eventually established mission stations in Africa, Asia, Greenland, Lapland and among the American Indians.

Student opportunity for influence—whether evil or good—is the same today. Someone will change history. The challenge is to follow Jesus Christ as He changes lives.

But who should go? Jesus of Nazareth chose followers who, though from diverse backgrounds, shared the enthusiasm, energy, teachability, flexibility and stubbornness of youth. He "called to him those he wanted," Mark writes in his Gospel. "And they came to him . . . that they might be with him and that he might send them out to preach" (Mark 3:13,14).

What is it about student-aged men and women that draws them so irresistibly to Jesus Christ and makes them responsive to follow Him in His great purposes? Throughout history, they are found on the frontlines of Christ's cause. Many of those listening to Jesus as He prepared to return to heaven were in that age-group. He said to them:

> All authority in heaven and on earth has been given to me. Therefore go and make disciples of all nations, baptizing them in the name of the Father and of the Son and of the Holy Spirit, and teaching them to obey everything I have commanded you. And surely I am with you always, to the very end of the age (Matthew 28:18-20).

The "Great Commission" is nothing less than God's heart to find people who are lost and scared and hiding. The Great Commission was given out of His passion. The task is not a hobby for missions specialists. It is a life-giving cause that is rooted in a relationship. It belongs to all of us.

Intimacy and Mission

In its intent, and in its means, the Great Commission is global and cross-cultural. It has always involved "all peoples on earth,"—from God's first words of covenant to Abraham in Genesis 12, to the day of the New Covenant of Pentecost in the second chapter of Acts when Luke records that people were present "from every nation under heaven," until the consummation of history in heaven's throne room where people from every tribe and tongue and people and nation who have been made "to be a kingdom and priests to our God" will worship Jesus Christ (Revelation 5:9,10).

The mission began before Christ was born when God made that eternal promise to Abraham:

> I will make you into a great nation and I will bless you, I will make your name great, and you will be a blessing . . . and all peoples on earth will be blessed through you (Genesis 12:2-4).

Dr. Ralph Winter, director of the U.S. Center for World Mission, writes, "In English, the word blessing implies merely a benefit—not also a relationship, as in the Hebrew *barak*. Americans, even American missionaries, typically do not understand the full significance of the privileges, obligations, and permanent benefits of the family relationship. Yet a relationship of just this significance is implied in the Hebrew *barak*. The implications here are profound, and exceed the normal intent of the evangelistic gospel. For example, in a family relationship you do not choose between evangelism and social action!"[3]

That blending of intimacy and mission captures the hearts of people who long for God to use their lives. It captures students.

The Original and Ultimate Missionary wanted our intimacy with Him and our sense of mission to be bonded, to be linked together. The ones He sent were to be, at the same time, both His beloved and the channel of His unmistakable focus and mission. Jesus was to be both the Enablement and the Companion.

It is significant to me that the German Moravians emphasized a personal relationship to Jesus as Lord as the central factor in life and ministry. "I have but one passion," wrote their leader as a young man. "'Tis He, 'tis only He." In the years since Count Zinzendorf led his co-laborers into the world, the university has proven to be a greenhouse for the disciples of Jesus Christ. You might even say that student-aged men and women have been God's chosen people in the work of missions.

Why? Because compared with their elders, students have fewer commitments and fewer regrets. Their decisions to follow Christ are often deep and far-reaching. In the last hundred years, as students have crossed borders to reach their peers in the great university centers of the world, their numbers have multiplied through generations of well-educated leaders in every country.

Now, sixty-six generations after those first followers of Jesus, student-aged people still seem to know that "being with Jesus" is the greatest feature of the Great Commission.

That integration of intimacy and mission strikes a special chord with college students today. Never has any generation been raised in such a global and cross-cultural context. Students are seeking a clear integration of that intimacy and mission, of grace and truth, as they represent Jesus Christ. Judging from the growing influence of students and from God's insistence that His Spirit give a unique anointing to each new generation, the last years of the

20th century may become known as "The Decade of Students."

Members of the powerful percent have always had a knack for recognizing, and at times orchestrating, the great turning points of history. Throughout the years, Christian students have held true to the deepest commitment of taking the gospel of Jesus Christ around the world. Their efforts have changed the lives of millions.

One by one, they have become runners in history's great "relay marathon"—the ongoing fulfillment of Christ's Great Commission. Allow me to introduce you to a few of my favorite examples.

Tell the students to give up their small ambitions and come eastward to preach the gospel of Christ.

> Francis Xavier
> to his Jesuit colleagues
> at the University of Paris
> From Southeast Asia, c.1549

Send us one of your best trained campus workers; trained in the school of failure as well as in that of success, that we may know that he will endure.

> A Missionary's Request
> From India, 1884

Christ for the students of the world, and the students of the world for Christ.

> Luther Wishard
> YMCA, 1895

Let us be satisfied with nothing less than leaving the deepest mark on our generation.

> John R. Mott
> Student Volunteer, 1910

There has never been a single regret . . . there has been no sacrifice, because the Lord Jesus Himself is my constant companion.

> Johanna Veenstra
> Student Volunteer, c.1930
> Missionary to the Sudan

It is my purpose, if God permits, to become a foreign missionary.

> The Student Volunteer
> Declaration

The decision to sign the Student Volunteer Declaration in my last year at Girton College, Cambridge, was the decisive moment in my whole life.

Ruth Rouse
Student Volunteer, 1948
(52 years after signing)

The will of God is always a bigger thing than I bargain for.

Jim Elliot
Student, 1950
Wheaton College

Win the campus today, reach the world for Christ tomorrow.

Bill Bright
President, Co-founder, 1951
Campus Crusade for Christ

< 2 >

The Marathon Relay Race

She stepped into the ministry before the close of the 19th century. During her years in India, she lost two husbands and three children. On the day we met, I was twenty-one years old and she was 103.

The only things I thought I had in common with Roberta Armstrong that day were a relationship with Jesus Christ and the belief that He had now called me to be a missionary, too. A missionary. Me, of all people. I'd only known Christ for two years, and that word was so laden with caricatures that I still tried not to use it very often.

As I walked into her room, I saw graciousness incarnate smiling up at me from a wheelchair. Her body was nearly useless, but that didn't seem to have the slightest effect on her energetic focus toward me.

Driving over that day, I had tried to think of some immensely profound questions. After all, this woman was a treasure house of wisdom and I knew our time together would be limited by her stamina. So, after the introductions and pleasantries, I knit my eyebrows into serious concentration and got to the point, "Mrs. Armstrong (she smiled so kindly that I almost forgot what I was going to say), why do you think God asked you to live so long?"

I didn't say so, but I was thinking that God hadn't treated her fairly. He could have at least worked it out so that one of her husbands or children could have outlived her.

She looked back for a long moment—eyes pausing somewhere between amusement and reflection. Then she leaned forward as if to tell me a big secret.

"Do you not know?" she inquired.

"Have you not heard?" she quizzed.

"The everlasting God, the Lord, the creator of the ends of the earth does not become weary or tired."

She stopped and smiled at me, not looking down on my youthfulness, but seeming to foresee some of what was ahead for me.

Then she confided,

> His understanding is inscrutable.
> He gives strength to the weary,
> and to the one who lacks might He increases power.
> Though youths grow weary and tired,
> And vigorous young men stumble badly,
> Yet those who wait for the Lord
> Will gain new strength;
> They will mount up with wings like eagles,
> They will run and not get tired,
> They will walk and not become weary.
> (Isaiah 40:28-31, NASV)

I was catching on. These words from Isaiah had been tried and found true by my pacesetters over the past 2,000 years. Mrs. Armstrong continued on through Isaiah 40 and 41 in a powerful and convincing narrative that left me persuaded as well. I was starting to be convinced that the Master I had only known for two years would be my faithful Companion also. I was beginning to believe that He would be both present and powerful over the course of my life and ministry, too.

I walked away that afternoon having seen the eagle in flight, wondering if eighty-two more years of walking with Christ might create such life in me.

Mrs. Armstrong finished her course not long after the day her encouragement and wisdom helped to launch me on mine.

The Race

You and I are runners in a great race.

In Seattle during the summer of 1990, a strong runner named Chuck Austin wrote to his children just before his death from cancer. From his perspective both as an athlete and as a Christian, Chuck told them that they, too, were runners in what he called a "marathon relay race." He used that metaphor to remind his children that their lives and ministries would require both the patience and stamina of a marathon, and the strategy and cooperation of a relay team.

Through the past 2,000 years, men and women like Chuck Austin and Roberta Armstrong who have encountered Christ deeply in their youth, seem to have been God's "chosen people" for taking the gospel of Jesus Christ into new frontiers. They haven't been God's only people, but they have demonstrated an unusual capacity for sensing His priorities and understanding how He can give ordinary people global and eternal influence.

The Runners

In the last one hundred years, it has become clear that as the message of Jesus Christ reaches the campus of today, the whole world feels the impact tomorrow. Nearly 2,000 years have passed since the apostle Paul settled into a personal ministry at the School of Tyrannus in the city of Ephesus. Fifteen hundred years later, the marathon relay was being run by Francis Xavier and the Society of Jesuits who founded universities from Ireland to Japan as a means of reaching the world.

Until the 1600s, most universities, whether Protestant or Roman Catholic, existed for one purpose: to train Christians. But even then, students were doing things their own way. They were organizing unofficial Christian societies, often in secret, perhaps to avoid ridicule or opposition from the religious authorities on their campuses.

The earliest reference to a student Christian organization in America was made at the funeral of a young schoolmaster in 1706. He had helped to create a Christian society at Harvard. Most of the Christian societies formed on campuses throughout the 1700s met for either theological discussion or personal encouragement.

By 1800, religious life in North America was dismal. Atheism and materialism flourished after the revolutions in America and France. Listening to some today who long for the values of the "good old days," you'd think that America in the last century was filled with devout church goers. In reality, only about 14 percent of the population was in church each Sunday. The situation on campuses was even worse.[4]

But in August 1806, the first student awakening of modern times emerged at Williams College in Massachusetts.

A group of five students had simply committed themselves to pray for revival among their fellow students. Each week they met south of the college in a meadow near the banks of the Hoosack River. One day they were just beginning their meeting when thunder clouds appeared in the western sky. Fearing a heavy storm, the group ran toward the campus. But when the storm proved to be only a shower, the students took shelter next to a haystack and continued their meeting.

Their leader, Samuel Mills, turned the discussion toward the world. "Come," he urged, "let us make (world missions) a subject of prayer under the haystack while the dark clouds are going and the clear sky is coming."

Out of this impromptu prayer meeting, a student missionary movement was created. The prayers and efforts of the group led to the formation of the first missionary society in America by 1810. By 1812, the first five American missionaries were on their way to India.

But in that year there were only twenty-five colleges in the country, with only a few enrolling more than a hundred students. With no telegraph, no railroad service, and infrequent mail delivery, Christian students on the different campuses faced virtually impossible odds in keeping in touch with each other.

The "Haystack Prayer Meeting" is marked by a marble globe monument erected at that site in 1856. It has come to symbolize the dream and vision for a major movement of students going overseas from the campuses of America.

By 1856, Young Men's Christian Associations (YMCA) began appearing on U.S. campuses. The stage was set. In the school year of 1875-76, a spiritual awakening began to take hold in the hearts of students at Princeton University. As a result, many of them traveled to other campuses to tell their stories. Thus was born the first intercollegiate Christian student movement in America.

In 1877, the YMCA formally organized a college division and appointed an 1876 graduate of Princeton as the first campus staff member. Luther

Wishard, fresh from his senior year at Princeton, took the job of directing the entire college work of the YMCA in the United States.

In 1878, Wishard heard for the first time the story of Samuel Mills and the birth of the American Missionary Movement. He then traveled to Williams College and there knelt in the snow at the Haystack Monument. He surrendered his own heart to the great Leader of those early volunteers praying, "I am willing to go anywhere at any time to do anything for Jesus."

Wishard returned determined that the YMCA adopt a strong emphasis on the Great Commission. He wrote:

> Let the students in these closing years of the century consummate what our fellow students in the earlier part of the century attempted. Let us engraft a missionary department upon this Intercollegiate Movement. We are their lineal spiritual descendants and successors; what they had begun it is ours to complete. They had willed, but our wills must now be brought into the plan to consummate their daring purpose.

The relay race grew and matured under Luther Wishard from person to person through the end of the 19th century. By 1884, he was receiving correspondence from his former YMCA students about the formation of student associations overseas. Speaking at a conference in that year, Wishard reported:

> At Tungchow College near Peking (Beijing) there is a band of students whose work, were it known, would be an inspiration to the entire

college world. Prayer meetings and Bible classes are maintained, individual evangelism is done in college and much preaching is carried on in the street chapels. A meeting is held every month to study the progress and pray for the spread of the Kingdom of Christianity throughout the world. Out of their bitter poverty these Chinese students are taking a hand in the evangelization of Africa by educating a boy in a school in Zululand at their own expense.

That fall, Wishard wrote a pamphlet on the Intercollegiate YMCA which pictured the building of a global movement. He wrote:

> The movement spread from Princeton College to two hundred other colleges, from America to Ceylon (modern Sri Lanka). It will continue to spread until the students in the missionary colleges in the Orient and in Africa are united with the students of America in one worldwide movement of Christ for the students of the world and the students of the world for Christ.

Finally, in 1886, Wishard's prayer for a unique awakening was fulfilled. That summer, with the help of the renowned Bible teacher D.L. Moody, he planned the first summer Bible conference designed exclusively for college students. Two hundred and fifty students arrived at Mount Hermon, Massachusetts, from ninety-six colleges and universities.

Although Moody did not plan to emphasize the Great Commission, within a few days he was persuaded to schedule a missionary program on two Friday evenings. On the second Friday evening, students presented the spiritual needs of ten nations. Those listening were deeply moved and hushed as they heard about needs in China, India, Persia (modern Iran) and Japan. The meeting closed, but many students prayed into the night, surrendering themselves to the lordship of Christ.

One who dedicated his life that night was John R. Mott, soon to be a junior at Cornell University. He described the mood of the conference in a letter to his parents:

> The Holy Spirit is working here with mighty power . . . Up to this noon, over 80 of the students have consecrated themselves to foreign missionary work and I know by Sunday night they will number 100. It thrills me through and through to record this fact. Here I have received a far richer anointing of the Spirit than I dared to ask for before I came.

By the last day of the conference, ninety-nine students had signed a missionary declaration which read:

> *We, the undersigned, declare ourselves willing and desirous, God permitting, to go to the unevangelized portions of the world.*

As they knelt in Crossley Hall during a farewell meeting, one more person opened the door and slipped in, filling the ranks of what came to be known as the "Mount Hermon 100."

The following school year, through the efforts of those one hundred students, more than 2,100 men and women volunteered for missionary service. By 1888, the missionary surge that started at Mt. Hermon became formally organized as the Student Volunteer Movement for Foreign Missions (SVM) of the YMCA and the Young Women's Christian Association (YWCA).

In 1888, Wishard knew that the European universities, and those of Great Britain, were eager to learn from the American experience and to encourage the growth of a Christian movement as indigenous to their national universities as was the student YMCA to American colleges.

In December of 1888, Wishard and his wife began a three-year tour to Japan, China, Malaysia, Siam (Thailand), Burma (Myanmar), Ceylon (Sri Lanka) and India. They traveled a thousand miles through the Middle East on horseback and then through Cyprus, Bulgaria, Greece, and Bohemia (Czechoslovakia).

They addressed thousands of students publicly, interviewed a thousand missionaries personally and spoke with scores of business and government officials. Thus, Wishard blazed trails, prioritized needs and prepared the way. But it was the Cornell graduate, John Mott, who was to provide the organizational spark.

From 1888 to 1894, Mott picked up where Wishard had left off in developing the U.S. student movement. In August 1895, he represented the United States in a plan to build the first worldwide student organization. To Mott the resulting "World Student Christian Federation" was "nothing less than the uniting of the Christian forces of all universities and colleges in the great work of winning the students of the world for Christ, of building them up in Him and of sending them out into the world to work for Him."

In the great years of ministry before World War I, there was among the students and churches, as one volunteer later wrote, the "feeling that we were one team, working for one world, under one Captain." Historians estimate that by the 1940s, more than

20,500 students who had signed the Mount Hermon declaration reached international assignments.

In the "Resources" section in the back of this book are some thoughts recorded by John R. Mott as an old man. They reflect some of the spirit of the Student Volunteer Movement.

My friend, Mrs. Armstrong, who began her turn in the race as a 19th century university student, was influenced by this movement.

In God's design, the legacy of the Student Volunteers led to the formation of new movements in the 1930s: The Navigators and InterVarsity Christian Fellowship emerged for a new generation of college students seeking to follow Christ into the world.

By 1946, InterVarsity formed its own worldwide student federation, called the International Fellowship of Evangelical Students. During the next thirty years, the IFES emerged as a leading Christian student internationale, with more than ninety national member movements and with staff pioneering in more than thirty countries.

By the 1950s, Campus Crusade for Christ was born in the minds of a couple of young entrepreneurs, Bill and Vonette Bright. Beginning at the University of California at Los Angeles, their goal was to "win the campus for Christ today, reach the world for Christ tomorrow." Within a short period of time, national leaders from Korea, Pakistan, Mexico and Finland had linked arms with the Brights. By 1991, the movement involved more than 100,000 college students and thousands of staff members in more than one hundred countries with plans to establish ministries on thousands more university campuses around the world.

The Lessons of the Race

As what Luther Wishard called "lineal spiritual descendants and successors" of this dramatic legacy, we have lessons to learn from the kindred spirits that have gone before us:

- There are moments when special energy and creativity come to a student generation. For a variety of reasons, these "windows of opportunity" may last for only a short time.

- The vision given in these special moments must be anchored in a movement of prayer. John Mott recognized this when he observed, "Prayer and missions are as inseparable as faith and works."

- Younger leaders, fresh from the campus are indispensable as pioneers of new ideas and new ministries. It matters little if they lack denominational ties or formal seminary training.

- The leadership of men and women together in a movement of God is crucial. Along with John Mott, the Student Volunteer Movement attracted a young English woman named Ruth Rouse. Finishing her studies at Girton College at Cambridge in 1891, she served first in India and then was appointed as a national representative for the Student Volunteer Movement in North America. In 1904, she was called to serve as the first woman secretary of the World's Student Christian Federation. From that post, Rouse traveled and spoke in the universities of pre-Revolutionary Russia and served more than forty years as traveling evangelist and encourager in campus ministry around the world.

- At the heart of a student movement of God is a single-minded focus on what John Mott called "a tremendously difficult" purpose. To the Student Volunteers, it was "the evangelization of the world in this generation."

- While focusing on the Great Commission, the men and women of the Student Volunteer Movement focused as well on the Great Commandment: to love our neighbors as ourselves. They took an early stand against racial discrimination, refusing to book conferences in hotels that practiced it and actively seeking interracial participation in their movement.

- While these student movements clearly spring from God's initiative, they portray the simple reality of ordinary people making extraordinary choices and sacrifices.

A Heart for the Race

In the autumn of 1895, Amy Carmichael, a young missionary from Northern Ireland sailed for southern India. In the ensuing five decades, she and the organization she built rescued hundreds of children from the painful humiliation of Hindu temple prostitution and led thousands of men and women to a relationship with Christ. She never returned home.

My tendency is to place people like Amy Carmichael into a category entitled, "disciples of biblical proportions." That way I can distance myself from uncomfortable comparisons. Unfortunately, she has not left that option open to me. Instead, she left volumes of her thoughts in writing. What I find in them are the heart desires of an ordinary young woman who was simply determined to know Jesus Christ very well.

What follows is a glimpse of how she prayed for herself. You may want to consider adopting her determined desire and tough ambitions as you step with Him into your own turn with the baton:

> *From prayer that asks that I may be*
> *sheltered from winds*
> *that beat on Thee,*
> *From fearing when I should aspire,*
> *From faltering when I should climb higher.*
> *From silken self, O Captain, free Thy soldier*
> *who would follow Thee.*
> *From the subtle love of softening things.*
> *From easy choices and weakenings.*
> *Not thus are spirits fortified.*
> *Not this way with the crucified.*
> *From all that dims Thy Calvary,*
> *Lamb of God, deliver me.*
> *Give me the love that leads the way.*
> *Give me the faith that nothing can dismay.*
> *Give me the hope that no disappoints tire.*
> *Give me the passion that will burn like fire.*
> *Let me not sink to be a clod.*
> *Make me Thy fuel, Flame of God.*
>
> **Amy Carmichael, India**

At first glance, it might seem like all the pioneering has been done. It may seem as though there is nothing now to compare with the life of Amy Carmichael or "with Ruth Rouse's journeys in pre-revolutionary Russia or with Luther Wishard's thousand-mile horseback ride across the Middle East"[5] . . . or is there?

The marathon is still on. And the baton has come to us. Our challenge is to seek the intimacy and experience the power and safety of a relationship with Christ. These are the things that marked those who have run before us. In their patterns of ministry, we find other elements of success in ministry too: cultural flexibility, imagination and inventiveness, and determination to address the deep needs and struggles of their own generation.

Part of our heritage reflects that, like them, we will run our own turn in our own way, no less empowered by the Lord of the Harvest, but in a way that reflects the uniqueness of life in this dramatic decade.

So the question is: What are the new ways of this new generation as its members prepare to take their marks?

There is never anything more important in the world than the work of the Church of Jesus Christ, and the most important work of any kind in the world today—greater than all of the problems facing men and nations—is the recapture of the great universities of the world for Jesus Christ.

> Dr. Charles Malik
> Former President
> United Nations
> Beirut, Lebanon

We need spiritual values, we need a revolution of the mind . . . we (now) say that the moral values that religion generated and embodied for centuries can help in the work of renewal in our country . . . All people have a right to satisfy their spiritual needs.

> Mikhail Gorbachev
> President, USSR
> the Vatican, 1989

< 3 >

The New Ways of a New Generation

I was praying that SwissAir would have a "no-talking section." Two weeks of intense cross-cultural communication had left me—as sociable as I am—a little bit wrung out. I had been discussing the concept of a worldwide network of students with some of my colleagues in Campus Crusade for Christ in Western Europe. The trip had been excellent. But now I was tired as I boarded my flight out of Basel, Switzerland, to London. Finding a no-talking section seemed like a reasonable prayer request. But then, there she was. Mrs. Gibby.

She was tall, elegant and English. And she recognized me from the flight over from London the previous Tuesday. Flying made her nervous, and could I assist her.

"Please?" she asked.

"Sure." I smiled, half out of politeness, half out of amusement. God had something in mind and, apparently, it was not the no-talking section.

As we began to taxi for takeoff, she stared out the window and anxiously twisted her hands, one around the other. I tried to distract her. "What brought you to Switzerland?" I smiled.

"My daughter is a student here." She risked a quick glance at me.

"Interesting," I observed, still smiling. "I work with university students."

As I explained what I do in my work with students, Mrs. Gibby turned slowly from the window and concentrated solemnly on my delivery.

Then she responded, deadpan, "During her time abroad, my daughter has become, I believe the term is, 'born again.'" Then she stopped.

What did that look mean? I wondered. I pressed on. "Mrs. Gibby, do you like the changes you've seen in your daughter?"

"As a matter of fact I do," she responded. "And she seems very happy."

You could probably make some safe assumptions about the content of the ensuing twenty minutes as we both talked about our lives. Somewhere over the English Channel I asked, "Mrs. Gibby, can you think of any reason why you wouldn't want to know Christ like your daughter does?"

"Ac-tua-ly," she replied in a way only the English can, pausing for effect, "no."

As a young Christian, Mrs. Gibby's daughter may have not yet discovered that she had thousands of Christian student compatriots around the world. Even so she apparently had been faithful to learn the truth, to live it, to talk about it, and to pray for others. Only she had done it in another culture—in Switzerland. In God's economy cultural, linguistic and political borders never seem to hinder the communication of the gospel. Cross-cultural communication seems to have always been a hallmark of Christian ministry.

On the flight from Basel that day, I had entered a story that was already unfolding. From what I could tell that afternoon, as we flew over Windsor Castle into Heathrow Airport, the mother of one of our fellow students finally gave her life to Christ.

I was left thinking about the Great Commission and about how my encounter with Mrs. Gibby had reflected the growing network of students in every country who are coming to Christ and talking about Him.

Changing Times

In many ways, the question marks and exclamation points of students are timeless. For as long as there are students, there will be late-night conversations about relationships and dreams and significance; about parents and jobs and sex and music and politics and all those other things King Solomon reflected on in his journal 3,000 years ago.

But in some ways, students do change. And that's what this chapter is about. Men and women like you that are twentysomething in these last years of the millennium have some pretty definite opinions and preferences. And as much as your thirty- and fortysomething friends hate to admit it, sometimes your ways are not our ways.

Problem is, those of us who like to think of ourselves as more mature are established leaders. We think our values and ways and means are tried and true and best. In fact, sometimes we think our methods are God's preferred ways of reaching this culture. We have acquired wisdom, and our commitment is to lead with it and to impart it—and hopefully, to stay teachable and listening through it all.

Personally, this is where I must come to grips with the true potential strength of the powerful percent. (Either that or I can just decide to not trust anyone under thirty.) You are, or will be, powerful in this generation because it is God's way to successively impart the fullness of His love and power and good intentions to each new generation.

"You, O Lord," wrote an anonymous psalmist, "sit enthroned forever; your renown endures through all generations." Jesus Christ reiterated that reality on the night before His execution when in praying for His disciples He said, "My prayer is not for them alone. I pray also for those who will believe in me through their message, that all of them may be one, Father, just as you are in me and I am in you. May they also be in us so that the world may believe that you have sent me" (John 17:20, 21).

He has used me and my generation. And by His grace, He will continue for several decades to come. And now He has created your generation and brought you, with all of the idiosyncracies of your slice of the American culture, to join us in the harvest. And now, together, we've got to ask ourselves, "What would happen if God arose, if He called and enlisted and empowered this generation of students . . .

"What could God do in a decade through a spiritually powerful percent?"

A Wake-Up Call

Some great campus ministries grew out of the magnificent work God did in the hearts of students forty years ago, and then again twenty years ago. But like most forty-year-olds, a movement like Campus Crusade for Christ will continue to grow only if the people in it continue to listen, both to the Lord and to the needs and questions and ambitions of their audience.

If the gospel really is the greatest news ever announced, it deserves the best communication we can give it. The gospel of Jesus Christ may have gotten your attention because of a relationship, a disappointment, or perhaps a dream or a frustration. Maybe you found the truth of God inescapable, or His love irresistible.

Our task as communicators begins with a deep respect for people and a desire to understand them, whether their differences are cultural, racial or generational. It's true "there is only one way to God, and that through Christ," but it is also true that when it comes to students, "there are a thousand ways to Christ."[6]

On December 31, 1999, we will celebrate the biggest New Year's Eve in history. And since the 21st century won't officially arrive until January 1, 2001, we'll have a full year to feel the impact of a triple-convergence: the end and the beginning of a decade, of a century, and of a millennium. The whole world will be watching. Between now and then, we will live out what *Megatrends 2000* called "the most important decade in the history of civilization, a period of stunning technological innovation, unprecedented economic opportunity, surprising political reform and great cultural rebirth."[7] I think there's a terrific chance that that secular prediction by John Naisbitt and Patricia Aburdene won't be remembered as wild overstatement.

Even though they share all of those splendid gifts of students from all generations, the college students of the '90s are showing up with minds of their own. As they were growing up, the boomers may have expected them to be yuppie clones, but they're not.

"There's a real clash of values in the workplace," observed one consultant. "The older managers think that if the shoe doesn't fit, you should wear it and walk funny. The baby-busters (i.e. twentysomething) say to throw it out and get a new shoe. Their attitude says that they are going to make the choices."[8]

Recently, I have listened as students have been accused (mostly by boomers) of apathy, selfishness, intellectual and spiritual shallowness, and of being spoiled. But I have kept listening to students, too. And I have come to the conclusion that God understands and works through the unique ways and insights of every succeeding generation. I hear great things from this generation.

One-Percent Factors

Students of the '90s have grown up with the liabilities of the formerly idealistic, hard-driving, have-it-all boomers. And not surprisingly, they have rejected some of the boomers' hallmarks. "Call it the boomer backlash," said a writer in *Fortune*. "The busters look around the office and observe the fortyish crowd, bleary-eyed managers who neglect their families and avocations for . . . what? By the time the boomers have made it, they've had it."[9]

As students today step up to their turn at making history, they bring with them some irresistible trends. They will change forever the organizations that are flexible enough to welcome them.

Those organizations can look forward to incorporating and even enjoying two great One-Percent Factors:

1. The last decade of the millennium will be the decade of the individual.

Workwise, graduates will be looking for a great personal fit. They will want to be certain that their life is making a difference. They will ask for ethical steadiness and strong communication and relationships with their co-workers and managers. And Christian graduates will be seeking authentic spiritual growth, that is, the kind that reflects emotional health. Twentysomething "busters" will be eager to develop their abilities and to get their hands on shaping the ministries that best express their burdens.

The trick for the "busters" will be to find a ministry that will help them to develop as leaders, while inviting them to participate in the creation and direction of the work, the ministry, which they choose. Organizations they work with must be flexible enough to benefit from their desire for individual significance.

But just as Christian movements will benefit, so will the newcomers. One of the most important tasks for those of you in your twenties is to experiment, to work hard at many things, to try on many "shoes" until by thirtysomething, you've learned enough to settle into a great long-term fit. There is a special advantage to spending one's first five years out of college working full-time with a well-run Christian ministry.

I know that sounds like a long delay in hitting the "fast track," but who wants to live the last fifty years on the wrong track?

It's interesting to note that God's pattern in discipleship, and in most Christian ministry, has always required this kind of twenties experimentation—in all dimensions of ministry. Because of that pattern, I'm personally grateful—now that I am, yes, fortysomething—to be doing things that God seems to have designed me for.

Here's a little thought-provoking secular analysis from *Megatrends 2000*:

> The great unifying theme at the conclusion of the 20th century is the triumph of the individual . . .
>
> It is an individual who creates a work of art, embraces a political philosophy, bets a life

savings on a new business, inspires a colleague or family member to succeed, emigrates to a new country, has a transcendent spiritual experience . . . Individuals today can leverage change far more effectively than most institutions . . .

"Mass" movements are a misnomer . . . (movements are) built one consciousness at a time by an individual persuaded of the possibility of a new reality.

As we globalize, individuals, paradoxically, become more important, more powerful . . .[10]

Since new arrivals will have high expectations, the veterans that will lead and develop them will need to be accessible, involved and authentic.

George Barna, author of *The Frog in the Kettle*, a Christian analysis of the United States in the '90s, writes:

Abdicating control over our lives is not something which we easily surrender. We respond best when we are involved in the decision-making process, when that process provides us with multiple choices and when the ultimate decision serves our own desires and best interests.[11]

With the growing focus on the significance of the individual, another One-Percent Factor is how that individual will relate to others:

2. The '90s will be the decade of the personal network: locally and globally.

These past forty years, ministries and businesses have tended to rely on the hierarchy, the chain of command, not only for direction, but for communication and motivation. Now, central control of institutions and movements is giving way to more personal and local communication, invention, experimentation, ownership and risk.

> The triumph of the individual signals the demise of the (centrally controlled) collective. Even Communists are persuaded that only the individual creates wealth. Within all collective structures (including organized religion)...there is the possibility of hiding from one's individual responsibility. At the level of the individual that possibility does not exist."[12]

The Scriptures clearly show that God gives men and women the responsibility to lead His enterprises. The Scriptures also affirm that the adult believer's "life-support system" is the diversity and mutual encouragement of the Body of Christ.

When an organization allows networking to become a principle means for the flow of communication and resources, the lessons of Ecclesiastes 4, Romans 12, 1 Corinthians 12 and Ephesians 4 begin to take hold. Networking tends to inspire another biblical value.

Jay Gary, missions author and trend watcher, pointed this out recently, "The final decade of the 20th century may well prove to be the greatest decade in Christian history for signs and wonders, miracles, conversions, evangelism, and the greatest wonder of them all: Christians loving one another and gathering in unity."[13]

In this age, so dominated by easy access to global communication and transportation, person-to-person contact within international movements will accelerate and broaden.

And just to make it easy on us, English is becoming more widely spoken than ever before. But that doesn't mean that any one country, even America, will ever dominate the world again. We will find our influence in partnership with our colleagues in other nations, and never again in paternalism.

As an individual becomes convinced of the significance of his or her work, and as he or she begins to build a personal, global network, the priority of relationships comes into view.

The Priority of Relationships

A Russian friend, Anatole, was talking to me recently about his most treasured possession.

"You know, Patricia," he said, "A Russian knows his life is a success if by the time he turns forty, he has established a circle of friends and colleagues that he knows he can trust and that he knows he can influence in life."

Anatole and his wife, Irina, are successful—they have their circle in Leningrad (St. Petersburg), and they have me in Seattle. Their network is local and it's multinational, and it's built on trust.

As one who thinks a lot about the future, I find Anatole's comment to be full of lessons about how to go about reaching the world in the '90s. Like Anatole, we Americans are starting to place a higher priority on relationships, especially as we carry out the Great Commission. That means that we will seek deeper levels of personal relationship, especially with our closest "teammates" whether we're in our home culture or another.

These two powerful forces, the growing desire for personal relationship and increased networking between individuals and ministries, could likely enable us to be "high-tech" and "high-touch" at the same time. Through our personal networks, we will be able to make sense of the volume of information and communication that comes to us. I find my focus, I give priority to the network of relationships that God provides for me, and I then trust God to extend my influence in the harvest far beyond my lone abilities.

A New Anointing for a New Generation

Today, students like you are not known, as were students of the '60s, for their "cause mentality." You are not as grandiose in your claims, and sometimes it's hard for you to name your heroes. On the other hand, you know what you want and you know what should change. You also know that one person can make a difference. You know that relationships are central to all of God's work, and you are comfortable in the roles of sensitive and curious pioneers, and of confident cross-cultural partners.

Given what's on the horizon, it almost seems like this generation of students has been tailor-made with some unique preferences and values, and then brought "to the kingdom for such a time as this" (Esther 4:14).

Worldwide Student NetWork:
Students of the World Reaching the World

OUR HEART: love for college students and confidence in them as they follow Christ.

OUR VISION: developing national leaders throughout movements of evangelism and discipleship.

OUR STYLE: teams in global partnership, aggressively going and sensitively serving.

< 4 >

The Roots of a Worldwide Network

In April of 1986, I found myself sitting in a room at Lake Arrowhead in Southern California surrounded by giant note paper taped to every wall. For three days, six of us talked and listened and argued and then illustrated our ideas on these big pieces of paper. By the time the walls were covered, we had come up with a few hunches about what God was beginning to do among the Christian students of the world.

Each of us, veterans of campus ministry with Campus Crusade for Christ, had become committed to a different part of the world. And since the early '80s, we had witnessed a tidal wave of students going on international summer missions projects. All over the world, students were making their mark—in Africa, Asia, Eastern Europe and the Soviet Union. Our unofficial networking on behalf of "our" parts of the world was resulting in some tremendous resources for the launching of new campus ministries.

Two other realities had built within each of us a sense of urgency about the role students could and would have in the world.

First, the Holy Spirit was speaking to us about the significance of the approach of the year 2000. Campus Crusade in cooperation with hundreds of churches and Christian organizations had begun work on "New Life 2000®,"* a comprehensive plan that could enable billions of people to hear the gospel

---

*New Life 2000 is a registered trademark of Campus Crusade for Christ.

and then begin to grow and be trained in the context of their own languages and cultures.

In light of that bigger picture, we knew that university-trained leadership would be needed in every nation. We knew that the global movement of students we envisioned would be fueled by the strong cooperation of Campus Crusade student movements in more than one hundred nations. We also realized that in light of the size of the task, our kindred spirits in like-minded student ministries based in churches and other Christian organizations would be a part of the network we envisioned.

On the wall on one of those big sheets of paper was a list of possible names for this movement. By the time we left, one name near the bottom of the list seemed right. That name reflected what we were faced with—a *Worldwide Student NetWork*.

I'd like to say that this meeting marked the invention of this vigorous young network, but I think it would be more accurate to call it the meeting that simply began to recognize a new work of the Lord of the Harvest.

In any case, as I got on the plane to return home to Seattle, I felt like a person who had just discovered fire. The sparks to take the gospel to every student, on every campus, in every country, had been within Campus Crusade for Christ and her partner ministries for years. But now God was leading us to dream of new ways in which to fan that flame, so that students all over the world might be ignited and united in the classic biblical philosophy of:

- reaching students with the gospel;

- building movements of multiplying disciples that would reach entire campuses; and through those movements,

- sending teams of students and graduates around the world.

As 1986 came to an end, the six of us at the Lake Arrowhead meetings decided to share this dream with Campus Crusade students at six Christmas Conferences across the United States. Thousands of students responded enthusiastically by collectively pledging more than $400,000 for the development of campus ministries among their counterparts in Asia, Japan, Eastern Europe, the Soviet Union and East Africa.

It was beginning to seem like the *Worldwide Student NetWork* was an idea whose time had come.

At first we were naive enough to think that this dream of building a network of students in the '80s, and casting it worldwide in the '90s, was something that God had put only into our American hearts. But as 1987 rolled around and we began to share this vision with our partners on other continents, we found that God had been giving similar dreams about a worldwide network to our staff, students, associates and volunteers from England to Germany, from Singapore to the Philippines, from Nairobi to Pretoria, and from Calgary to Buenos Aires.

Then, before too much longer, we discovered that what God was showing us had already struck a chord in the hearts of hundreds of like-minded associates: students from Christian colleges, other university ministries, and church-based college ministries. We had potential partners everywhere with the same desire to reach their peers in other nations. Soon, we were explaining the vision and the needs to our associates. They began to respond. We could be full partners: They had mature Christians to equip and send, and Campus Crusade ministries around the world had an overall plan that came in bite-sized chunks.

Jesus often used fishing analogies to communicate what it meant to be a part of a movement of evangelism. In Matthew 13:47, Jesus said, "the kingdom of heaven is like a net." Webster's Dictionary defines a net as "a fabric made of cord, loosely knotted or woven in a pattern to catch fish." A good metaphor. God was beginning to prepare that kind of net, linking us together and releasing our resources, to reach the students of the world for Christ.

The Unfinished Task Among Students

As we began to look at the challenge before us, we knew that one of our first steps was to get a better picture of the magnitude of the unfinished task. We needed answers, and good ones.

In June of 1987, we embarked on a quest to cast new light on the size and scope of the work ahead. With the help of Jay and Olgy Gary, we were able to use state-of-the-art technology to develop the University Database. Before long we had the world's most extensive information about campuses and their students.

Soon Jay and Olgy were analyzing this new data. From their analysis the *Student Evangelism Index* emerged—a ground-breaking tool that compared the need for student evangelism among the countries of the world.

College Students Worldwide

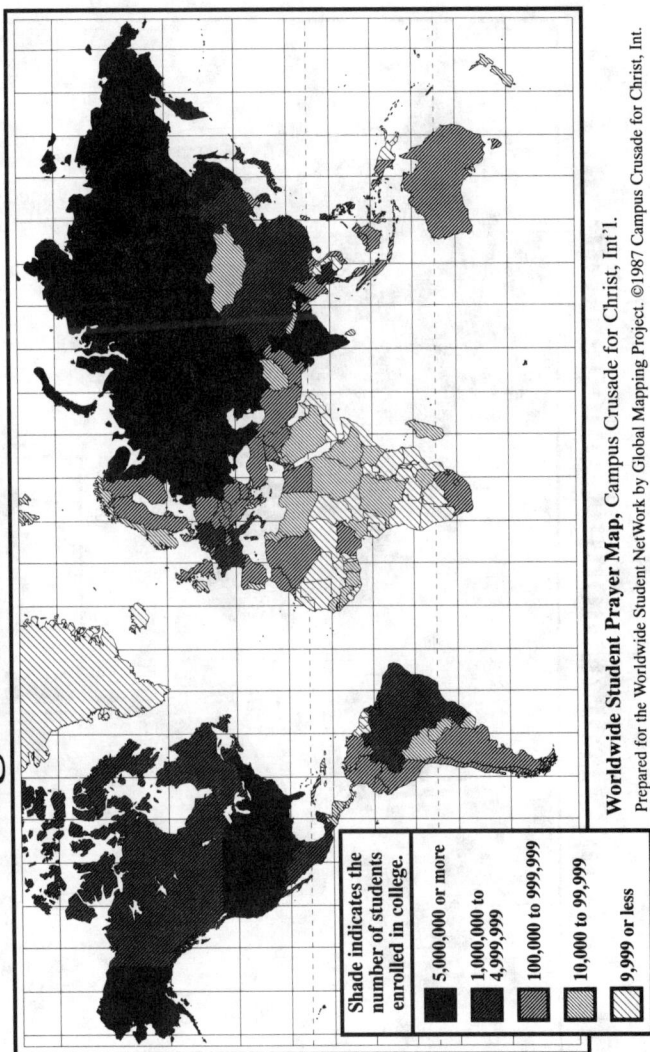

Shade indicates the number of students enrolled in college.

- 5,000,000 or more
- 1,000,000 to 4,999,999
- 100,000 to 999,999
- 10,000 to 99,999
- 9,999 or less

Worldwide Student Prayer Map, Campus Crusade for Christ, Int'l.

Prepared for the Worldwide Student NetWork by Global Mapping Project. ©1987 Campus Crusade for Christ, Int.

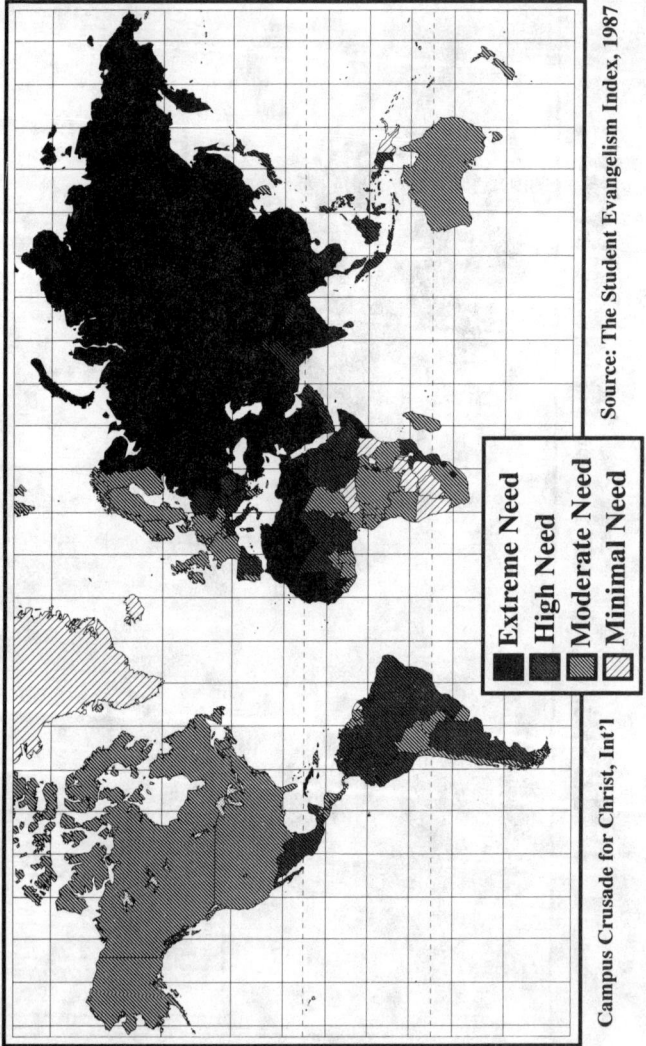

Evangelism Among College Students

Campus Crusade for Christ, Int'l

Source: The Student Evangelism Index, 1987

Extreme Need
High Need
Moderate Need
Minimal Need

Here is what the *Student Evangelism Index* revealed in four categories:

- *Extreme Need:* These twenty-eight countries were considered "unevangelized." They represented 32 percent of the college-student population, or approximately 17 million students.

- *High Need:* Forty-two countries were considered "slightly evangelized." They represented 28 percent of the world's students, about 15 million.

- *Moderate Need:* Next in line were fifty-nine countries which were identified as "moderately evangelized," representing 39 percent of the world's student population, about 21 million.

- *Minimal Need:* The thirty-two countries which scored lowest in the index were considered "generally evangelized," representing less than 1 percent of the world's students.

What else did our information reveal? Some of the news was astounding.

In some countries, the winning, building and sending of college students was bearing fruit a hundredfold. In parts of sub-Sahara Africa, 10 percent of the student body was involved in discipleship groups. The same was true for selected parts of Asia and the Pacific, such as Singapore.

In other areas the news was sobering.

Today, despite the efforts of so many denominations and student ministries, more than one-third of the world's college campuses do not have access to any Christian staff workers.

This is especially true in the Muslim world. From Morocco to Pakistan, only a few universities enjoy a viable witness to Muslim students.

In secularized Western Europe and North America, hundreds of campuses have had local ministries for years, but still have no sense of movement and impact.

When you turn to the French-speaking colleges in Africa, a majority are still in the pioneer stage. The news also revealed the same is true in the universities of China or North India.

Further, we were reminded that since each year brings nearly a 25-percent turnover in student populations, our plans had to be highly flexible and long-term in their intent, but aggressive as well.

As we studied the *Student Evangelism Index*, it looked like we were on the right track. For years, God had led us to go into many of the countries listed under the extreme-need quadrant.

We were beginning to get a clearer focus on the scope of our task. But we needed even more information.

"Take a Census of the World!"

This is where Roger Randall, one of the original paper hangers at Lake Arrowhead, stepped in. Since his days as a student leader, Roger had served in many leadership positions with Campus Crusade in the United States, including seven years as the national campus director. But in 1985, Roger and his wife Sara had set forth on a new adventure. They had begun to travel three to four times a year to sub-Sahara Africa to conduct training conferences for staff involved in campus ministry. It was no coincidence that the ministries there were enjoying a spurt of growth!

In three years, the results had been dramatic. The effectiveness of students and staff in building movements of evangelism and discipleship had so improved that the establishment of ministries on every major university campus in Africa had become a reachable goal—even by the mid '90s.

As the spring of 1988 rolled around, Roger sensed that the Lord wanted more than just a census of Africa. As the Lord had once commissioned Moses to number the men twenty years old and upward who were able to fight (Numbers 26:1,2), Roger felt that God was now telling us to *take a census of the world*.

As Roger explained his idea with leaders around the world, they agreed. Using the information in the University Database, fact sheets were created for every country of the world, listing the major universities. These computer printouts were then sent to staff in more than one hundred countries to help them determine the status of our global campus ministry. We also began to learn more about the dreams of these staff and students for their countries and continents.

The results of the "Worldwide Campus Ministry Census" started to trickle in during the spring of 1989. By the fall of that year, an incredible 80 percent had responded. Roger's census had revealed some encouraging results.

By 1991, we had learned that Campus Crusade for Christ was ministering on nearly 1,100 campuses, with the potential to directly reach one out of five college students around the world. And these statistics still hadn't factored in the great work of God through other local and multinational ministries. Amazingly, 40 percent of our campus works had been started since 1984. We were indeed a young movement!

As we began to look forward to the '90s, we started to ask ourselves, What could God do in a decade through a spiritually powerful percent?

How Do You Eat an Elephant?
"One bite at a time."

Though there may be as many as 25,000 colleges, vocational institutes and universities around the world, more than 90 percent of the world's students are enrolled in just 4,000.

Students on these key universities share many of the same characteristics, yet these universities are incredibly diverse.

Many schools are in typically "open" countries like Thailand, Japan, and the countries of Western Europe where the barriers to ministry are similar to those in the United States. In other countries, access to key campuses is limited by political or religious restrictions.

Some campuses are a challenge because of their vast or minute sizes. In Argentina, Mexico and Thailand, literally hundreds of thousands of students attend the national universities. However, in India, the average size of a campus is under 5,000 students.

The challenge is even greater in most industrialized countries where there are few strong models of movements on large urban campuses.

The 8,000 major universities and colleges worldwide can be divided into three main groups:

Level 1
This level includes about 1,500 schools, about 1,000 of which are outside of the United States. These are the key national universities and colleges of the world. With three- and four-year-degree programs, their enrollments usually exceed 5,000

students. Fifty percent of all college students worldwide can be found on these "hub" campuses. What could God do in a decade? Our desire is to help equip each of these campuses with a team of full-time staff.

Level 2
This includes about 2,500 schools, with an average enrollment of under 5,000 students. Around 42 percent of all college students worldwide attend these institutions. In many places where schools are too small for a full-time team, the staff at nearby Level 1 campuses are reaching them through local relationships.

Level 3
This includes about 4,000 campuses that are attended by 8 percent of the world's students. As smaller community-based colleges, their enrollments are usually less than 1,000 students. Because of the size of these schools, overall community and city strategies are the best resource for reaching these students with the gospel.

The Umbrella
Faced with all of these needs and numbers, we became convinced that the vision of a worldwide student network was bigger than any amount of central planning and control could handle. We could gather information and sharpen our focus, but ultimately we had to unleash this generation of students with:

- their genius for pioneering
- their desire to serve as teams
- their determination to work internationally via personal relationships and cultural sensitivity, and

  • their resources of communication and trans-
    portation.

By the summer of 1988, the *Worldwide Student NetWork* was becoming an umbrella under which resources and opportunities could meet and partnerships could be built. Campus Crusade for Christ may have helped to build the foundation, but Campus Crusade ministries were not along under the umbrella.

What would God do in the decade of the '90s? We began to watch as the concept of international partnerships began to grow.

Two of a Kind: International Partnerships

By the end of 1991, the University Database had been used to create an even more comprehensive picture of where we stood and where we needed to go. Computer technology was used to bring the information to a level where more of us could use it. It had become a creative and captivating program called "C.T.'s World Tours" (named for the famous Cambridge overachiever and Student Volunteer, C. T. Studd). Students at conferences were beginning to explore their hunches and opportunities by moving a computer's mouse across a colorful screen.

Besides finding out whether the country they had their eye on had a McDonald's near campus (really, it's in the program), they began to discover that four hundred Level 1 schools in twenty-two countries were without viable campus ministries. And in each case, national leaders were asking for our help in launching new student movements.

About half of those four hundred schools were culturally and politically most accessible to American involvement (after all, we were reminded, American ministries weren't the only "sending" ministries). After further discussion with international leaders, fifty of those schools became our most immediate focus as American campus ministries.

Once our focus was clear, we could get serious about creating many more partnerships between sending American ministries and key international universities.

We found that the best partnerships were simply groups of people who together possessed enough resources to launch and build a partner ministry on a key campus in another country. That usually means that partnerships are formed by clusters of campus ministries, or by combinations of Campus Crusade chapters and local church ministries.

For people considering what their partnership could look like, here are two important issues to consider:

- Are we focusing on the best opportunity?
- Are their enough of us:
  . . . to send three to five year-long teams (on a program known as *STINT*) until full-time staff are in place,
  . . . to send annual summer mission projects,
  . . . to develop on ongoing prayer movement to support our partnership,
  . . . and to help fund the growth of the new ministry, and
  . . . to ultimately help send a full-time resident team that will work alongside national staff.

As a student committed to a partnership ministry, actually going to your partner nation might be one of your first steps or your ultimate goal. But a partnership involves many other dimensions. It means aggressively praying, preparing, giving and then going too—as long as possible or as often as possible.

In the past few years, some of the best expressions of partnership have been through what have become known as the "bridges of responsibility."

From Bridges to Beachheads

In 1987, students and staff in Kansas, Missouri and Nebraska began committing themselves to a long-term partnership with students in Hungary. As they talked about ways of expressing their partnership, they came up with the following "bridges of responsibility" that have since become hallmarks of the WSN:

1. Pray

First things first. They began to pray for the countries that were most on their minds. They prayed for spiritual awakening, national healing and changed lives. They followed the conventional wisdom on learning to pray: they simply started talking to God personally and with a few like-hearted friends. Soon, their prayers began to focus on a special partnership that God was preparing for many of them. God put Hungary on their hearts.

2. Give

Soon they were beginning to help finance specific projects that would contribute to the growth of the ministry. Student leaders from Hungary began to show up in Kansas for training.

3. Go

Of course, they began to go, together, from their home campuses to what was then Communist Hungary. At first, scores of students and Campus

Crusade staff members went for a summer. They were joined in their partnership by the strong college ministry at the First Evangelical Free Church of Fullerton, California. Before long, God had called a handful of the finest leaders in their ranks to make a permanent move to Hungary.

4. Personalize

They took a personal interest in everything about Hungary. We admit it, this is a catch-all category. "Personalizing" has meant everything from learning about the partner country's history and culture to paying attention to what's making their headlines. It may also mean learning the language of that country. This category also includes the best bargain in a cross-cultural experience—reaching out to 360,000 international students who study in the United States each year.

5. Mobilize

The men and women of Kansas, Missouri, Nebraska and Fullerton learned a valuable lesson. They decided to cross each of these bridges together, not as heroic individualists. Increasingly, small groups of friends began to pray and prepare together, especially as they considered going together.

They pioneered a pattern in the *Worldwide Student NetWork.*

The depth and breadth of their partnership with Hungary resulted in a steady flow of short-term projects in both directions. Perhaps most significantly, the partnership has led to the decision of several Americans to move long-term to Hungary, learning the language and working alongside young Hungarian leaders to help create a vigorous movement of God in Central Europe.

The pattern of their partnership has spread through the scope of the WSN, not only to local and statewide Campus Crusade ministries, but to WSN associate ministries. Via networking among Americans, students from the First Evangelical Free Church of Fullerton, for example, have joined the pioneers from the Midwest in forming their own long-term partnership with Hungary.

A partnership is a big commitment, so by God's design, it is begun in the climate of prayer and relationships.

If you haven't settled on a specific national group of students to which you will be committed, start praying, learning, and giving with a heart open to God. The Lord of the Harvest will patiently give you the specifics.

A few resources to help you create a partnership and then to start crossing bridges can be found in the back of this book in the section entitled "How Can We Connect?"

Keeping Perspective

This could get overwhelming if we were unaware of what God has done through students in the past, if this was strictly an American enterprise, or if everything didn't ultimately rest on the ever-powerful, ever-loving Lord of the Harvest.

The marathon relay has been marked by the special work of God among students who prayed and who became convinced that He could use them, and did.

And today partnerships are pioneering new movements and providing resources for those which are already established. Creative initiative and friendships are spawning a fabulous climate for the exchange of vision, resources and the necessary follow-up of new believers and new ministries.

It's been said that when one person dreams—it is a dream; when many people dream together—it is the beginning of reality. Very quickly their dream begins to spread. The *Worldwide Student NetWork* may have gotten an initial boost here in the United States, but now it is thoroughly a matter of "students of the world, reaching the world."

It has only been four months since I became a Christian, and I want to advance faster in my walk with Jesus.

I want to begin a new ministry on my campus where there is none now.

My future direction after graduation is to work for God in Japan.
Japanese students

In these days we are really happy, we are full of energy, hope. Hard times are coming, but we'll live with the help of the Lord and the faith in our Creator.
A Russian student

I have been convicted that Africa must rise up and take its challenge of missions. We cannot afford to wait for the total evangelization of Africa before we reach out to the rest of the world.
Peter Assimwe
Campus Director, Uganda

Students try to encounter an abundant life in the political system, but that is something only Christ can give. I believe this is true not only for students, but also for all the people of Honduras and the entire world.
Norman Lenin Hernandez Galo
Honduras

The only thing I have to look forward to is getting to know God and the Bible . . . I will continue until I am old.
A Chinese student

If these drastic changes can take place in such a short time, why can't we really believe God to do the impossible and reach our country for Christ?

An Eastern European student

< 5 >

Partners in 85 Nations

In December of 1983, I was in Leningrad. It was cold. President Ronald Reagan had just labeled the Soviet Union "the evil empire," and glasnost wasn't even in the realm of imagination.

My partner and I were in town for a couple of weeks to contact students who had been introduced to Christ the previous summer by Western students on the project we had dubbed "Northstar."

We had been interrogated and followed and frustrated all the way through Moscow and Kiev. Leningrad was our last stop, and we were hoping these few days would run more smoothly. After a long walk on a cold night to ensure we had not been followed, we waited in the shadows of an old cathedral-turned-museum for a young woman named Olga and her boyfriend, Sasha.

Then there they were, striding toward us and grinning as if we were their oldest and dearest friends. I think they had already decided that we could be. Russians are like that.

After the introductions, we walked back to Olga's apartment and told each other how we had come to know Christ. It had only been six months, but these two had a vibrant faith and were eager to grow. How had they grown so much without Bibles? They were evidence to me of the Holy Spirit's faithfulness and of the privilege it is to have a small part in His plan.

This was the night that we would give them Bibles for their very own. We dug into our bags and pulled out two complete Bibles and handed them to Olga and Sasha. They responded as if it were

Thanksgiving, Christmas and the Fourth of July all rolled into one great celebration.

As we introduced them to the treasures they held in their hands, we asked them to find the Book of James. We explained why James had written his epistle, to whom and when, then we began to read together the first chapter. They had plenty of questions about trials, perseverance, wisdom, prayer, mortality and temptation. But at one point, the issue of faithfulness took the spotlight.

"In English," I told them, "'Faithful' can mean two things: It can mean 'responsible,' and it can mean 'filled with trust.'" Then I asked, "What does it mean in Russian?"

Without hesitation, Olga leaned forward with her eyes reflecting calm determination. "Faithfulness," she said simply, "is the attitude of a servant who is prepared to die for her master." (And we were teaching them?)

Sometimes I think my hope for the fulfillment of the Great Commission is built on moments like that.

As we talked late into the night, as Russians do, I was mindful that these two had been raised in an environment of militant atheism. I realized that they had lived all their lives with the same frustrations I had been experiencing for two whole weeks and that, unlike me, they weren't going to be able to leave in a few days. They had heard the gospel of Christ through fellow students, and now they fully expected to know Him and to make Him known just as aggressively.

When it was time to go, they walked with us for awhile. Just before they left us, Olga got that determined look in her eyes again, kissed her new Bible, and said, "If you will keep coming, and if you will keep teaching us, we will teach many others."

And on a cold winter night in Leningrad, the foundation of what was becoming a worldwide student network grew by two.

Seven years after my evening with Olga and Sasha, in the autumn of 1990, the first full-time resident campus team went to work in Leningrad. British and American staff and students went to work alongside young Russians like Olga and Sasha, and a new campus ministry began to flourish.

As the gospel spreads from student to student around the world, newer members catch the vigorous faith of those who have led them to Christ.

In the breathtaking scope of the *Worldwide Student NetWork*, there are opportunities that students can pursue better than anyone: reaching their peers, launching campus ministries, and developing leaders for the work of Christ in their home nations and beyond. Many of the men and women giving national and continental leadership today were student leaders only a few years ago.

Here are few of my favorite stories of their adventures from around the world.

From Japan

In the summer of 1983, two hundred American students and staff members went on an initial summer missions project to Japan. They were cautioned by experts that the Japanese didn't naturally understand spiritual things and were slow to trust or make decisions. "Go to Bible school, learn the language, study the culture. Then begin your ministry," the experts advised.

But with a summer to experiment and armed with some good training in reaching their peers, these students walked onto campuses in Japan and did what came naturally. Within six weeks, more than a hundred Japanese students had indicated interest in trusting Christ and had joined a Bible study. By the end of the summer, twenty of the Americans phoned home and made arrangements to stay on through the school year.

When I visited Tokyo in 1985, I met a young student named Junko who had known Christ for six months. Junko spoke English already and was now majoring in Russian. On a long shot, I asked her, "Would you ever consider sharing your faith in the Soviet Union?" Not only would Junko consider it, but the following summer, she flew to New York, went through a project briefing with an American team, flew with them to Moscow, and spent the summer sharing her faith in her third language. Show off. Junko has since joined the staff of Japan Campus Crusade for Christ.

From Eastern Europe

While some of the first Campus Crusade staff members were preparing to move into Eastern Europe, "a maverick American university student named Joe was paving a way for them. Joe decided in the early '70s that he didn't have to wait for graduation to head overseas as a missionary. He'd heard that his Polish heritage guaranteed him admission to a university in Poland, and when he packed up his things for Krakow, he threw in copies of the *Four Spiritual Laws* booklet and other materials on the basics of Christianity that he'd used while involved with Campus Crusade in the States."[14]

Once in the country, Joe showed copies of those materials to Cardinal Karol Wojtyla who gave his blessing for them to be used among Polish Catholic students. Who but God could have known that

Cardinal Wojtyla was soon to become Pope John Paul II.

"Joe later met Father Franciszek Blachnicky, who was directing a grassroots movement of young people. Their goal: restoring a personal relationship with Christ to the heart of the Catholic religious heritage claimed by 90 percent of Poles.

"Joe asked Father B if he would be interested in meeting American Christians working with a world-wide, non-denominational missionary agency that had the same goals. Father B assented enthusiastically, and Campus Crusade was brought unofficially but momentously, into Soviet-controlled Europe."[15]

In the years that followed, teams of gifted veterans of campus ministry moved to Poland from the United States and Western Europe. From small beginnings, they succeeded in helping to open new ministries in Central Europe. And each one quietly relished the fact that on June 1, 1991, the ministry in Poland became officially recognized as The Great Commission Movement, and sixty full-time Polish staff members were leading it. It should now be no surprise that like the Americans that first went to their country, these young Poles have begun to reach out to other nations, planning summer missions projects to places like Tbilisi in the formerly Soviet Republic of Georgia.

From China

By May 1, 1989, the pro-democracy movement in Beijing's Tiananmen Square had begun to lose momentum. It wasn't until student leaders urged urban workers to join the protest that the movement reached its height. Once it had, the troops and tanks moved in.

"In the aftermath of the Beijing massacre, a student leader named Li, responsible for organizing urban workers, found that his dreams were crushed. Fearing arrest and even the loss of his life, he rushed to give an evacuating foreign teacher a letter for his wife and son studying in Canada, instructing them not to return to China.

"That same evening, he hesitantly received from the foreign teacher a copy of the well-known explanation of the gospel, 'Power for Living,' but said that he didn't believe in God. Six months later, it was learned that not only did Li become a Christian, but he copied the article eleven times so he could share with other student leaders the real truth he had found in Jesus Christ."

Li's response to the gospel is not uncommon. It can be a long process for a Chinese student to accept Christ, but when he or she does, they frequently begin sharing their faith with others without hesitation. Because of this tendency, the government has been warning students about the "Christian fever" that is sweeping their university system.[16]

From Zaire

Central African students at the University of Kinshasa in Zaire have concluded that the name "Campus Crusade for Christ" is too tame. So they've decided to call themselves "Commandos for Christ." During one exciting period of ministry, 220 commandos had shared Christ with more than 1,500 of the 12,000 students on their campus. The response has led to discipleship groups in every dorm, daily classroom meetings during their noon break, and the involvement of forty to fifty professors and administrators in small group Bible studies.

From South Africa

In a visit with three extraordinary South Africans, I learned that the ministry in their country was started by a handful of Americans in the late '70s. But today, the ministry staff of thirty-five includes only three non-South Africans, and the racially-mixed teams and movements reflect every cultural group. My three friends jokingly refer to themselves as a "culture club" because of the curious responses they tend to get about their highly public, interracial working relationships.

See if you can follow this: Douglas Jansen, a so-called "colored"[17] campus director, with his mainly non-white team, leads the mostly-white ministry at the racially-mixed University of Witwatersrand in Johannesburg, a campus of 18,000 students. Did you get all that? Here's what Douglas has to say:

> There are lots of tensions at this stage between the various racial groups, but we find that this brings an opportunity to our ministry. As brothers and sisters in Christ, we can show what it is for the races to work together.
>
> We would like to see all our students involved in full-time work sometime in the future. First of all, as a movement we'd like to be representing Christ in the way we work together as Christians, not only in reaching our immediate campus, but also moving out to the rest of Africa, and reaching Africa for God. Together, we are committed to Africa.

Cookie Jansen, Douglas' wife, a so-called "colored" associate campus director, agrees:

> Our country is known to be in upheaval. There are many changes economically,

politically and socially. But in spite of it all, we as staff have found that the basic and consistent need is for people to have a relationship with God.

Their friend, white Afrikaaner Wynand Lindeque, is the campus director at the University of Pretoria. He adds:

> We as Afrikaans-speaking students and staff on that campus have a big role to play in the future of our country. With the many changes that have been going on in South Africa, there is a need for a new example to follow. As Christians, we can set an example for everybody to see that it is really possible to work together toward the goal of reaching the world for Christ. That's the only solution for any problem, and for all mankind.
>
> Our campuses represent the many cultures of South Africa, so what better place is there to start?

In recent years, these leaders have coordinated inner-city and rural projects and have begun their own spring-break outreach called "Operation Sonshine" on the beaches at Capetown. In the summer of 1990, forty-five students and fifteen South African staff joined a multinational project working on the campuses of metropolitan Manila in the Philippines.

From Latin America

As a student in Bolivia in the turbulent 1960s, Rolando Justiniano wanted to change society. His vehicle was Marxism. His weapons were hate and violence.

"In street battles with the police," he says, "my buddies began falling dead and wounded around me. But I noticed a curious thing—it was never the leaders that died. They were always behind the lines somewhere. I began getting disillusioned with radical groups."

About that time, Rolando met two Campus Crusade staff members, a Bolivian and a North American, who began to talk with him about Christ.

"Soon God replaced my hatred for people with love," he writes. "When I met up with Campus Crusade, I saw they really wanted to change the world. They were reaching key leaders of the country—those in the university."

Rolando received Christ and was soon speaking out about his faith. A few years later, a young woman named Carmelita attended a meeting at which Rolando was the speaker. She found herself captivated by the teaching that God loved her. Eventually, she placed her faith in Christ, too.

Then one day, a few years later, she married the speaker.

Now Rolando and Carmelita direct *La Cruzada Estudiantil y Profesional para Cristo* throughout Latin America. As the '90s began, their staff of three hundred were working in twenty-one countries, including Cuba. And twenty-three new staff members, all recent university graduates, had just joined them.

"These new staff inspire me," says Rolando, "for in Latin America only a small percentage of the population graduates from a university."

The ministry in Latin America is growing rapidly and establishing key partnerships with campus ministries in Texas, Colorado, New Mexico and Arizona. The ministry at the University of Costa

Rica is led by students with what one of their North American partners calls "a determined, ordered purpose." Valmore and Anita Shaw lead a movement of two hundred fellow students. Valmore schedules his classes so he can pray and meet with disciples in the morning, share his faith every afternoon, and attend classes three nights a week.

From The Middle East

Historically, almost nothing interrupts movements of God among students as much as wars between nations. World War I threw sand in the gears of the Student Volunteer Movement, and in August 1990, students around the world, especially in the Middle East, had to again deal with the prospect of war.

Just months before the Iraqi invasion of Kuwait in the summer of 1990, students involved with Campus Crusade at the University of Amman in Jordan traveled into Iraq to show the "JESUS" film. (The film is based on the Gospel of Luke and is used around the world in evangelism strategies.) In September of that year, these same hundred students found thousands of refugees on their country's border with Iraq. Bringing food and the message of God's love, they headed for the desert to help meet the needs of these uprooted people.

And in one of the most ironclad of the Islamic republics, full-time national workers, though unable to communicate with the rest of us, are pressing on, reaping much fruit. Their work must be discreet. In the past two years, eight thousand men and women have become Christians and 75 percent of their ministry is supported financially from within the country.

From Russia

The ministry to students which grew for so long in secret, is bursting with great joy and fruitfulness in the climate of freedom which has marked the beginning of the '90s.

In September of 1990, the first year-long (a.k.a. STINT) teams of American and Western European staff and students moved into Leningrad and Moscow. Their task was to work with Russian student leaders to help build a strong Christian movement.

Working together that fall with key Russian students, these young British and Americans helped to organize huge gatherings in a Leningrad sports stadium. For three consecutive nights in October, crowds of 22,000 came together as a Finnish staff member presented the gospel with an invitation to trust Christ. On the third night, the meeting was televised, reaching an estimated audience of 70 million Soviets.

This letter soon arrived in Seattle from a wonderful young American serving in Leningrad:

I cannot sufficiently word how I felt at the end of the first meeting when the speaker asked people to come forward if they wanted to express their new belief in Jesus Christ. As I had my head bent down in prayer—it was not the anxiety of hearing the clear foot fall of single human beings, but the immediate reaction of thousands, literally at least half the stadium, coming along the aisles! A herd of cattle might have passed quieter!

Tears still come to rest in my eyes when I think of the small glimpse of heaven I was privileged to see—so many confessing belief! And the hope that these new Christians need in this country, oh that they may be filled with it! So many putting trust in God to make a difference.

My prayer is that God would be that difference in their hearts and lives, that they may be the difference in this country and world . . .

And the following note arrived from a twenty-year-old Russian friend who served as the translator for the meetings:

Hello Patricia!

I haven't written for a while because of my being busy. I'm sure you're somehow well-informed about the great event, "Mission Leningrad '90." I had a lot of things to do during the mission and before it as I was translating for the preacher.

Every Christian could contribute into the mission and we've done it well but the real work just starts, for during the three days many people, to be correct, thousands and thousands of them repented and expressed their will to accept Christ as their Lord and Savior. That means that now we've got plenty of work to be done. The harvest is plentiful and laborers are few. And the work has just started.

I want to tell you also that in our university, there are regular Bible study groups. It's exciting, and even I'm not afraid to say that it is unbelievable, miraculous. People become more and more open, and here is a real hunger for God. Things are changing, and we feel this is the answer to the prayers of many brothers and sisters here and abroad.

We have here American students who are really a great help. If I were able, I would pour down on you all my excitement and happiness, but I think this is something too difficult to express.

Come here, Patty, you'll see a lot of amazing things. One Christian revealed to me why I have to live on this earth for some time instead of going to my Father right away. The reason is that I'll bring many other people with me, helping them to see the glory of my Lord.

With much love and greetings from my friends,

Andrei

By the fall of 1991, Leningrad was again called "St. Petersburg," and the numer of American and Western European STINTers serving alongside their Russian partners had tripled.

One thing we can be assured of: the *Worldwide Student NetWork* is not a theoretical American invention.

In the summer of 1990, five hundred leaders associated with the *Worldwide Student NetWork*/Campus Crusade for Christ in scores of countries met in Manila, Philippines. They included:

- warm and flamboyant staff members from Trinidad and the countries of Africa;

- delightful and candid Latin Americans;

- quiet, gracious (and slightly mysterious) former Hindus from India;

- men and women from the Middle East— intense about Christ and about proclaiming Him to their Arab countrymen (also, I thought, the owners of the best smiles);

- bright and earnest East Asians;

- enthusiastic Eastern Europeans still relishing their new freedoms;

- and a few very encouraged North Americans and Western Europeans.

"Before Manila I was trying to reach El Salvador," a Latin American leader writes, "but now I'm working to reach the whole world."

It was a gathering at which everyone was a minority, and at which the apostle Paul's goal that we be "united in spirit, intent on one purpose" (Philippians 2:1-11) was a reality. I came away fully convinced that in partnership with these incredible disciples, we are seeing a great and growing movement of evangelism and discipleship among students of every nation.

The two principle tasks of the *Worldwide Student NetWork* in the coming decade will be to help strengthen established ministries and to pioneer new ones. These things will happen as we pray, give, reach international students on our campuses, learn a second or third language, and as we help other students learn to do the same.

And, of course, some of us will cross the ultimate bridge and *go* to the world. As we will see in the next chapter, there have rarely been so many exciting avenues and options.

In Kiev, where I found myself on a Sunday morning (in 1933), on an impulse I turned into a church where a service was in progress. It was packed tight, but I managed to squeeze myself against a pillar whence I could survey the congregation and look up at the altar. Young and old, peasants and townsmen, parents and children, even a few in uniform—it was a variegated assembly. The bearded priests, swinging their incense, intoning their prayers, seemed very remote and far away. Never before or since have I participated in such worship; the sense conveyed of turning to God in great affliction was overpowering.

Though I could not, of course, follow the service, I knew . . . little bits of it; for instance, where the congregation say there is no help for them save from God. What intense feeling they put into these words! In their minds, I knew, as in mine, was a picture of those desolate abandoned villages, of the hunger and the hopelessness, of the cattle trucks being loaded with humans in the dawn light. Where were they to turn for help? . . .

Every possible human agency was found wanting. So, only God remained, and to God they turned with a passion, a dedication, a humility impossible to convey. They took me with them; I felt closer to God then than I ever had before, or am likely to again.[18]

Malcolm Muggeridge
reporting on the famine in
the Ukraine under Stalin

Ask yourself: if there is something you supremely want to do, do you count as self-sacrifice the difficulties encountered or the other possible activities cast aside? You do not. The time when you deliberately say, "I must sacrifice this, that, or the other" is when you do not supremely desire the end in view. At such times you are doing your duty, and that is admirable, but it is not love. But as soon as your duty becomes your love the self-sacrifice is taken for granted, and, whatever the world calls it, you call it so no longer.[19]

Dorothy Sayers
The Whimsical Christian

That which I heard I forgot, that which I saw I remembered, but that which I experienced became part of me for the rest of my life.

Proverb

< 6 >

The Third Bridge

Have you ever noticed how, in the way He asked questions, Jesus had a way of gently but irresistibly getting to the point?

In His gracious style, Jesus Christ could move people from the philosophical to the personal.

On the way to Caesarea Philippi one day, He asked His disciples, "Who do people say I am?" He may have seemed casual, nonchalant, academic, even theoretical. And the disciples responded with mental speculation.

When they had finished expounding on the first question, Jesus had another. With one small change, He switched emphasis from their minds to their hearts. "But what about you?" He asked. "Who do you say I am?"

"What About You?"

Nothing moves a discussion about the Great Commission from the theoretical to the personal more quickly than a question about the third bridge, the bridge of personally *going* to the world: "What about you?"

In talking about what it means to be in a partnership with students in another nation, we've talked about the five bridges of responsibility:

1. *praying* regularly;

2. *giving* financially;

3. *going* for a month or a lifetime;

4. *personalizing*—learning about your partner country's present situation, history, culture and language; then

5. *mobilizing* your friends to do all of the above.

This chapter focuses on the special, personal drama of crossing the third bridge.

Although going to another culture is only one of five bridges, in a way it stands alone.

We're about to get personal as we consider the magnificent implications of actually taking your well-prepared soul to the world.

Basic Training

In the tenth chapter of Luke's Gospel, Jesus nudges seventy-two of His disciples out of the nest, all at the same time. Here's what happened:

> After this the Lord appointed seventy-two others and sent them two by two ahead of him to every town and place where he was about to go. He told them, "The harvest is plentiful, but the workers are few. Ask the Lord of the harvest, therefore, to send out workers into his harvest field. Go! I am sending you out like lambs among wolves. Do not take a purse or bag or sandals; and do not greet anyone on the road.
>
> "When you enter a house, first say, 'Peace to this house.' If a man of peace is there, your peace will rest on him; if not, it will return to you. Stay in that house, eating and drinking whatever they give you, for the worker deserves his wages. Do not move around from house to house.

"When you enter a town and are welcomed, eat what is set before you. Heal the sick who are there and tell them, 'The kingdom of God is near you'" (Luke 10:1-9).

Talk about getting thrown in the deep end! Look at the essence of those instructions again: *On this assignment,* Jesus told them, *there's lots to do and there's only a few of you. Don't take extra money, luggage or shoes . . . and don't spend all your time in random evangelism. Go to specific groups of people. Oh, and there'll probably be some personal rejection mixed in with the miracles.*

After a few more instructions about how to handle opposition, the seventy-two were on their way. And before long, Luke records they were back. They "returned with joy and said, 'Lord, even the demons submit to us in your name'" (Luke 10:17).

In listening to their good report, Jesus rejoiced, too, but then He reminded them, "Do not rejoice that the spirits submit to you, but rejoice that your names are written in heaven" (Luke 10:20).

We can learn some important lessons from the instructions of Jesus to these people. Did you catch them?

- Ultimately, you can't just be taken to the world, even by a special movement of God. *You have to personally initiate.* It's your choice.

- *Going requires innovation.* As we have seen, the seventy-two could take no extra money, luggage or shoes. Their mission was to reach specific groups of people and not spend all their time in random evangelism. Obedience was going to take some thought.

- Rejoice in the ministry, but no matter how good it gets or how many miracles you see, remember that your ultimate joy is in the certainty of your own splendid salvation. *Don't ever think that going to the world will improve your standing with Jesus Christ.* That's already a settled issue: He's crazy about you.

As the chapter continues, a lawyer "put Jesus to the test," asking Him, bottom line, what was required to inherit eternal life. When Jesus answered with patient questions and quiet affirmations, the lawyer persisted, "trying to justify himself." This time he wanted to know, once and for all, "Who is my neighbor?"

Lawyers and experts on the law didn't always get such a patient and quiet response from Jesus. I've wondered if this man might have been one of the seventy-two. People who sign up to go to the world don't magically stop "putting Jesus to the test." Nor does the human urge to "justify themselves" leave them.

The first chapter of James invites people like you and me to ask our questions, promising that God will give wisdom, "generously and without finding fault." God wants us to feel so safe and uncondemned around Him that we will ask our questions with candor and honesty. He happens to know that candor and honesty lead to authentic growth. Maybe James could write those words because he had spent years watching his older brother, Jesus, patiently answer honest questions.

In defining "neighbor" for the lawyer, Jesus told the parable of the Good Samaritan:

A man was going down from Jerusalem to Jericho, when he fell into the hands of robbers. They stripped him of his clothes, beat him and went away, leaving him half dead. A priest happened to be going down the same road, and when he saw the man, he passed by on the other side. So too, a Levite, when he came to the place and saw him, passed by on the other side. But a Samaritan, as he traveled, came where the man was; and when he saw him, he took pity on him. He went to him and bandaged his wounds, pouring on oil and wine. Then he put the man on his own donkey, took him to an inn and took care of him. The next day he took out two silver coins and gave them to the innkeeper. "Look after him," he said, "and when I return, I will reimburse you for any extra expense you may have" (Luke 10:30-35).

A neighbor, Jesus wanted the lawyer to know, is likely to be a person from another cultural, political, religious or economic background. The work of a disciple with a "neighbor" is to take the initiative and to show compassion.

Going to Your Neighbors

During the 1980s, nearly 1,000 U.S. Campus Crusade for Christ staff and close to 10,000 students and their associates from churches and other ministries went to the world on short- and long-term mission projects. Equipped with the principles and skills of personal ministry, with basic cross-cultural training, and with a special part to play in a global drama, these men and women have helped create new ministries to students on every continent.

"Sending" ministries and their partners have discovered scores of creative ways to serve one another. As a result, the best opportunities to cross the third bridge reflect various lengths of time.

Question: What are the options?

A. *U.S. and International Summer Projects—eight to ten weeks*

This is the most popular first step.

Campus Crusade Summer Projects in resort areas and university centers of North America and other countries have demonstrated that they not only give a great initial exposure to ministry, but they make strategic contributions to the long-term development of a national campus ministry. Since historically these projects have been in places where national students spend their summers, they have played a major role in helping to break new ground and to build scores of new relationships.

The genius of a summer or semester-long project is that they are linked to an ongoing ministry. Both national workers and long-term American staff can pick up where the short-term teams have to leave off. Frankly, without that kind of an established context, short-term international ministry can look more like "hit and run" religious tourism.

As with all *Worldwide Student NetWork* projects, a primary ministry audience is English-speaking university students. Even so, some teams spend a portion of each day studying the language of the nation in which they serve.

Going short term is just about the best way to discover if a longer term assignment (three to five years) would be a good fit for you.

B. *STINT (Short Term International)—a full school year, two semesters abroad*

Since the mid-1980s, we've been asking young, well-equipped teams to set up shop in key areas of the Middle East, parts of Asia, Eastern Europe, Latin America and the republics of what used to be the Soviet Union. After spending a year working as a team and launching and building a campus ministry, many STINTers sense a deep conviction about returning for an even longer stay. If you've been involved in helping to lead a campus movement of evangelism and discipleship here in the United States, you have some idea of what a STINT team can do in a year.

C. *Long-term international assignments—three years to life*

As with most ministries here in the United States, Campus Crusade's long-term goal is always to help raise up a permanent on-site team. Unlike short-term opportunities, men and women on long-term assignments take time to learn the national language as a means of ministry.

The goal for any long-term team is to help reach and build national students to become leaders, assuming major responsibility and ultimately leadership in their own national ministry.

Question: How do we prepare?

Consider the options, both in light of the strategic needs of your partner country and in light of the development of your local ministry. Then start crossing bridges:

- Begin a prayer movement on behalf of a potential partner nation, then

- Start to develop a team of men and women who will commit to crossing bridges with you. Each of these "going" options requires a strong ministry background. In addition to good ministry skills, these projects tend to demand flexibility and emotional stamina. So you won't be surprised to hear that men and women who are most effective in their ministries are committed to prayer, depending wholly on God, and relating and communicating with each other.

- Become further equipped in the skills of campus ministry. You will want to become familiar with the philosophy and goals and materials being used in the country you're going to. The materials you will use in the national language will utilize the same principles that work among students in the United States.

- Start now to build relationships with the international students on your campus who are already facing the challenges of crossing bridges into a new culture. Every year 360,000 international students are drawn to American universities. Many of these students have come looking for new insights about the issues of life. And many of them

will return to positions of leadership in their
homelands. Amazingly, during their years in
the United States, these same students will
be quiet and studious and often ignored, even
by those of us who care so deeply about
reaching their nations.

Question: How do we connect with the greatest needs?

For a complete list of who to call for ideas about
anything from getting started locally to establishing a partnership, to applying for STINT or a
summer project, check out the "How Can We
Connect?" pages at the end of the book.

It's been 2,000 years, but the Lord of the Harvest
still calls, instructs, sends and rejoices with His
laborers. And, I've noticed, He's still sending them
out by teams rather than all by themselves. The
needs and opportunities are stunning, so let's take
a closer look at how you can get spiritually ready to
go.

Creative imagination and power are released just in so far as the world purpose of God is realized and accepted, and the will of the individual or of the community is brought into line with that purpose. Those alone have clarity of vision who see the world as God sees it.

> Ruth Rouse
> Student Volunteer Movement

The will to win means nothing without the will to prepare.

> Juma Ikangaa
> Tanzania
> Winner, 1989
> New York City Marathon

Christianity works incredibly well at 100 percent, and is painfully frustrating at any other level.

> Gary Stanley
> International School
> of Theology

Lord, You take the pen, and the lines dance. You take the flute, and the notes shimmer. You take the brush, and the colors sing. So all things have meaning and beauty in that space beyond time where You are. How, then, can I hold back anything from You?

> Dag Hammarskjold
> *Markings*

I shall be telling this with a sigh
Somewhere ages and ages hence:
Two roads diverged in a wood, and I —
I took the one less traveled by,
And that has made all the difference.

> Robert Frost
> "The Road Not Taken"

< 7 >

A Road Less Traveled

The Great Commission is not a hobby for the really religious. It belongs to anyone who realizes he is called to follow Christ. Personally, my favorite part of the Great Commission is where Jesus says, "Therefore go . . . and be sure of this—that I am with you always . . . " (Matthew 28:19,20, TLB). God the Father is the Originator of the great redemptive plan, Jesus Christ is both the Cornerstone of the plan and our highest Example, and the Holy Spirit is our Power to live and serve as God asks. Through Him, we experience the love of God, and because of His loving power to change lives, Jesus called Him the "Lord of the Harvest."

And in our obedience, though the Great Commission is our highest purpose, the Great Commandment is our truest way. Life is relationships. And personal ministry, as God designed it, teaches us more about Christ's love through the lives of people who love and serve Him along with us. So our preparation for this "road less traveled" begins with relationships. In relationships, to God and to our teammates, questions find answers:

- How and when will I know I'm "called to go"?

- What am I good at? What are my personal and spiritual gifts?

- How will I ever raise enough money?

- How can I make sure that I will serve with a mature and supportive team?

- How will I be to my teammates what they need?

- How will I know where in the world God wants me to give my heart?

- How will my vision, involvement and heart for people look when I'm forty years old?

- Will I keep learning about God's grace even as I'm busy giving my life in ministry to others?

- How will my closeness to Jesus Christ feel after twenty more years of this?

- How will my personal desires fit in with this world vision?

"Whose Servant Will You Be?"

That question was a vital issue in the mind of Jesus. More than anyone else in the New Testament, He talked about what it meant to be a servant. Several words for "servant" were available, but Jesus kept homing in on the Greek *doulos* (doo-laas).

In the first century, that word designated a class of the most lowly slaves. But when Jesus used the term, He flooded it with love. When He called someone a *doulos*, He was driving home a point: The fulfillment of a commission must always be linked to the intimacy of a *doulos* with his or her master.

Probably as a result of that focus, every writer of a New Testament letter used it as his personal claim to fame:

- Paul, a *doulos* of Christ Jesus, called as an apostle, set apart ... (Romans 1:1)

- James, a *doulos* of God and of the Lord Jesus Christ ... (James 1:1)

- Simon Peter, a *doulos* and apostle of Jesus Christ . . . (II Peter 1:1)

- Jude, a *doulos* of Jesus Christ . . . (Jude 1:1)

- The Revelation of Jesus Christ . . . to His *doulos* John . . . (Revelation 1:1)

As the apostle Paul wrote from prison in Rome to his persecuted friends in Philippi, he, as usual, began by referring to himself as a *doulos*. Then with a stunning illustration, he explained the secret behind his joyful tenacity. The God he loved and served had taken on Himself "the very nature of a *doulos*, being made in human likeness" and had become willing to render the ultimate service (Philippians 2:1-11). Paul could keep going because he had an intimate relationship with a divine Master who not only directed and empowered, but who had gone before and understood anything Paul or his friends would have to live through.

An Ordinary Jewish Girl

The first chapter of Luke's Gospel gives the account of still another *doulos*. The story is of an ordinary Jewish girl, living in an ordinary Jewish town:

> In the sixth month, God sent the angel Gabriel to Nazareth, a town in Galilee, to a virgin pledged to be married to a man named Joseph, a descendant of David. The virgin's name was Mary. The angel went to her and said, "Greetings, you who are highly favored! The Lord is with you.

Let's say you're brushing your teeth tomorrow morning and all of a sudden a brilliant Presence tells you something like that? What would you say? We're not sure that Mary could choke out much of anything. All Luke gives us is one of those great biblical understatements: "Mary was greatly troubled at his words and wondered what kind of greeting this might be."

Have you ever noticed how just about the first thing these messenger angels have to say to people is, "Calm down!"? (Remember the shepherds?)

> But the angel said to her, "Do not be afraid, Mary, you have found favor with God."

The angel continues, and he unloads a lot of news:

- You will be with child and give birth to a son,

- and you are to give him the name Jesus.

- He will be great and will be called the Son of the Most High.

- The Lord God will give him the throne of His father David, and

- he will reign over the house of Jacob forever;

- and His kingdom will never end.

This ordinary Jewish girl living in an ordinary Jewish town had a question. I think it was a logical one: "How will this be, since I am a virgin?"

Remember how Jesus responded to the lawyer and how James promised that God would answer honest questions? That's the kind of reply that Mary got from the angel: "The Holy Spirit will come upon you, and the power of the Most High will overshadow you. So the holy one to be born will be called the Son of God . . . For nothing is impossible with God."

Mary had come to God often and knew Him well before this time. All you have to do is read her song of praise later in Luke 1 to know that she had made a point of knowing the Scriptures, of knowing her Master. And now she heard His word directly.

For years her roots had dug down deeply into knowing Him, so now she said the only logical thing: "I am the Lord's *doulos*. May it be to me as you have said."

Mary had come to God often, she had heard His word, and she knew to how to trust in His power to see His plan accomplished.

And she called herself a *doulos*. In the understanding of a citizen of first century Galilee, a *doulos* was:

- one who was born or sold into slavery;

- one who was bound to his master as his personal servant;

- one whose will was swallowed up in that of his master.

Under Roman law, a *doulos* was in a permanent involuntary relationship to his master. That bond could only be broken by death. There were no limitations about the nature or length of his service.

Under Hebrew law, the rules were a little different. Normally, a Hebrew servant was released after six years. There was only one condition under which Jewish law permitted complete and lifelong bondage. The condition is defined in Deuteronomy:

> If your servant says to you, "I do not want to leave you," because he loves you . . . and is well off with you, then take an awl and push it through his ear lobe into the door, and he will become your servant for life. Do the same for your maidservant (Deuteronomy 15:16, 17).

Slavery went out of style a long time ago, so citizens of the 20th century might need a little help with the concept of living voluntarily as a *doulos*.

It seems to me that it means:

- living with your eyes on a Person in a strong relationship;

- experiencing life as you sense His presence and power;

- acting on His directions, invitations, requests and desires, and knowing all the while that

- service is a two-way expression of love.

Whose Doulos?

Living by faith only makes sense when you see yourself as a *doulos* in a relationship with your Master.

Even though slavery is out of fashion, you and I tend to be slaves by virtue of the fact we're human. The Bible speaks of slavery to wine (Titus 2:3), to sin and impurity (Romans 6), and to "false teachers who promise freedom, while they themselves are slaves of depravity—for a man is a slave to whatever has mastered him" (2 Peter 2:19).

The implications seem clear: We probably will serve somebody or something. The catch is that any master other than Jesus Christ will sooner or later become a tyrant. Paul wrote to his disciple, Titus:

At one time we too were foolish, disobedient, deceived and enslaved by all kinds of passions and pleasures. We lived in malice and envy, being hated and hating one another. But when the kindness and love of God our Savior appeared, he saved us, not because of righteous things we had done, but because of his mercy (Titus 3:3-5).

Faith works when you understand that Jesus Christ is the Master and you are His beloved *doulos*, that you can trust Him when you give your life to Him—just like Mary and some of the people you've read about in these pages.

The essence of the Great Commission is the part where Jesus Christ promises to be at the center of the pursuit, not only the heart behind the command to go, but the one who would enable and encourage us in the task.

When we begin to feel confident about our abilities as leaders and communicators, especially when things are going well, it's easy to forget who it is that can bring satisfaction to our souls.

Genesis 22 tells the story of a man I would have liked very much. His name was Abraham. He loved his son Isaac fervently. God tested Abraham to determine whether he loved Isaac as a gift or as an idol. God's command must have fallen on Abraham's ears like the blows of a hammer:

> Take now your son.
> Your only son.
> Isaac.
> Whom you love.
> And sacrifice him as an offering.

How would you fill in these blanks concerning the things or loved ones in your life? "Take now your _____, your only _____, _____, which/whom you love . . . and sacrifice it/him/her as an offering."

Could it be:

- your hard-earned college degree? The business you love?

- your closest relationship?

- that dream of finally winning your father's approval? Your central dream, the one for which you'd give anything to see fulfilled?

Could you sacrifice it/him/her as an offering?

You probably know that the story of Abraham and Isaac has a happy ending. Abraham learned an important lesson: His beloved Isaac could not be the focus and center of his life.

What are you tempted to place at the center of your life? What/who is your first love? Is it:

- a dream you've never talked to God about?

- the rush you get from listing your achievements and affiliations?

- the desire to finally win the approval of your parents?

All these things are great gifts, but they're lousy gods. In fact, if they are at the center of your life, they can get tyrannical.

Once you've settled the issue of who your Master will be, your next task is to stay centered on Him.

The Apostle Paul's Pilgrimage

A tough old missionary, Paul saw himself as a *doulos* of Jesus Christ. He kept Christ first, and as a result, he experienced the deep affection of his Master. Even so, there were times that life became grueling for Paul. In light of that, I've been curious about the secrets to his staying power. He never quit.

Shortly after he left his lengthy ministry at the School of Tyrannus at Ephesus, Paul recounted for his friends in Corinth some of the tough times he had lived through:

> We have this treasure (the gospel) in jars of clay (our bodies) to show that this all-surpassing power is from God and not from us. We are hard pressed on every side, but not crushed; perplexed, but not in despair; persecuted, but not abandoned; struck down, but not destroyed (2 Corinthians 4:7-9).

> As servants of God we commend ourselves in every way: in great endurance; in troubles, hardships and distresses; in beatings, imprisonments and riots; in hard work, sleepless nights and hunger; in purity, understanding, patience and kindness; in the Holy Spirit and in sincere love; in truthful speech and in the power of God; with weapons of righteousness in the right hand and in the left; through glory and dishonor, bad report and good report; genuine, yet regarded as impostors; known, yet regarded as unknown; dying, and yet we live on; beaten, and yet not killed; sorrowful, yet always rejoicing; poor, yet making many rich; having nothing, and yet possessing everything (2 Corinthians 6:4-10).

> Five times I received from the Jews forty lashes minus one. Three times I was beaten with rods, and once I was stoned, three times I was shipwrecked, I spent a night and a day in the open sea, I have been constantly on the move. I have been in danger from rivers, in danger from bandits, in danger from my own countrymen, in danger from Gentiles; in danger in the city, in danger in the country, in danger at sea; and in danger from false brothers. I have

labored and toiled and have often gone without
sleep; I have known hunger and thirst and have
often gone without food; I have been cold and
naked. Besides everything else, I face daily the
pressure of my concern for all the churches
(2 Corinthians 11:24-28).

Apparently the guy didn't know when to quit!

In many ways, Paul was just like you and me as a
runner in the marathon. A little over a year after
writing these things to believers of Corinth, Paul
wrote his letter to the Romans. Hidden away in a
corner of this, his Magna Carta, was a clear explanation of his personal staying power.

The Apostle Paul's Staying Power

The year was A.D. 57. With twenty years down
and perhaps ten years to go, middle-aged Paul was
still going for it. In his letter to the Romans, he got
personal with his friends:

I have written you quite boldly on some
points, as if to remind you of them again,
because of the grace God gave me to be a
minister of Christ Jesus to the Gentiles (unbe-
lievers) with the priestly duty of proclaiming
the gospel of God, so that the Gentiles (unbelieving people) might become an offering accept-
able to God . . . (Romans 15:15,16).

Paul taught that God's ever-loving grace belonged
to everyone who said "yes" to Jesus Christ. Knowing
we're forgiven and no longer condemned, we learn
freedom and confidence to grow.

Like Paul, our steady, wholehearted boldness to
serve the needs of unbelieving people grows out of
our love for Christ.

By God's design, students possess the gifts of enthusiasm, energy and sheer stubbornness. With those gifts of youth, come a natural sense of seeking to achieve, to perform, for acceptance. From what I can tell, this is true of students everywhere.

The problem is that grace is designed to free us to be used powerfully, not as a reward for performing powerfully. Until that becomes clear, it's natural to think of the Christian life as a goal or a program—an "it." But God's grace makes sure that we never forget the Christian life is "Him."

On the night before His death, Jesus prayed, "This is eternal life: that they may know you, the only true God, and Jesus Christ whom you have sent" (John 17:3).

The more Paul understood that his mission to serve God was an intimate expression of love, to know Christ better, the more his call captured not only his mind and his imagination, but his heart.

The first secret to Paul's staying power was the understanding he had of grace: *his Master's grace was the source of his boldness to initiate ministry.*

Paul records the second reason for his tenacity in Romans 15:

> So it is right for me to be a little proud of all Christ Jesus has done through me. I dare not judge how effectively he has used others, but I know this: He has used me" (Romans 15:17,18, TLB).

At this point in his life, Paul also was experiencing *the unique satisfaction of knowing that God had worked through his efforts.* God's eternal priorities became Paul's temporal ones.

Then the apostle gave a third reason for his staying power:

Through the power of the Spirit . . . from Jerusalem all the way around to Illyricum (today this area is called Albania), I have fully proclaimed the gospel of Christ. It has always been my ambition to preach the gospel where Christ was not known, so that I would not be building on someone else's foundation. Rather, as it is written: "Those who were not told about him will see, and those who have not heard will understand" (Romans 15:19-21).

By "fully proclaimed," Paul meant that in his preaching he had "fulfilled, perfected, consummated, and made (the gospel) complete in every particular." In translating "fulfilled," one commentator says that it means Paul's ministry had "given the gospel its full development so that it has reached every quarter."[20]

I believe in this passage the great apostle was implying a three-fold commitment to the Great Commission:

- First, geographically. The description he gives of his "turf" included all peoples who had never seen nor heard of Christ in all the world of the first century.

- Second, theologically. Paul's desire was to fully proclaim the gospel of Christ. This meant not only giving enough information for a conversion, but the building of disciples who would grow thoroughly and authentically in grace and truth.

- Third, lifelong. Paul meant "fully" in terms of the length of his life. Although his youth was in the distant past by this time, he could envision no greater adventure. The grace of

God had recharged his imagination, and he was smiling at the future.

Your choices have brought you this far. They have required courage and tenacity. Your influence for Christ is growing—both deep and wide. The question is, will you continue passionately? Faithfully? Students all over the world are having to answer that question. Many live under tougher circumstances than we have here in the United States.

The kingdom of God initiates, it is expansive, bold and deep. Those qualities overflow from the work of His Spirit, the Lord of the Harvest, in the lives of people who grow in the sweet lessons of Romans 15.

On July 31, 1976, seven young leaders in the U.S. Campus Ministry were killed in the flood of the Big Thompson River in Colorado. In the weeks before her death, one of the women had been considering the scope of what God had called us to do together. Speaking of the way God works through students, our friend would say, "If the New Testament were still being written, I bet we'd be in it!" I bet she was right.

The Challenge

The way of faith is a road less traveled. But perhaps you've stuck with me this long because, well, in the words of Jesus, you might be a laborer. Out of 12 million American college students, maybe you are a *doulos*. If so, the road less traveled will require you to keep seeking Jesus first, then enjoy the safety of staying close to Him and become skilled in communicating His grace and truth.

You will want to consider the possibility of at least a season—maybe the first three to five years of your post-graduate career—in full-time ministry, here or overseas. If your intent is to walk fruitfully with Christ for the coming eighty or so years, you will want to become skilled at understanding the priorities and ways of God and aware of the questions and needs of people. In the process you'll learn much about the way God has designed you for Himself.

Many who come will stay for only five years before moving on. But those years will help you to be effective with people for the rest of your life.

Years spent in ministry promise everything Paul mentioned in Romans 15:

- a chance to learn of the grace that gives safety and thus boldness and courage,

- an experience with the deep personal significance that comes from pursuing what God says are first things, and

- a chance to have your imagination charged with the sheer scope of the Great Commission.

Don't Go Alone

Remember, it was Francis Xavier who wrote around 1549 to his colleagues in Paris, "Tell the students to give up their small ambitions and come eastward to preach the gospel of Christ."

A "small ambition" could simply mean making wrong choices out of a confused image of God, or centering your life on things that won't matter 10,000 years from now.

Who do you know who is learning to identify and put away small ambitions? Who is learning about grace and following Jesus Christ in the central issues of life? Who do you know who is learning to stand up strongly but kindly for what he/she believes? Have

I just pictured any of your closest friends? I hope so. Have I just described any of the people you've dated in the last year? I hope so.

You were never designed to walk alone down this road less traveled. God has for you some fellow servants—people with whom you will work hard, laugh long and take risks. They will be your closest compatriots and deepest influencers. If you're still on the road when you're old, it will be because you walked with people like that.

So. Will you be a *doulos* for life? It's strictly your choice, you know:

> If your servant says to you, "I do not want to leave you," because he loves you . . . and is well off with you, then take an awl and push it through his ear lobe into the door, and he will become your servant for life (Deuteronomy 15:16,17).

You may want to pause here and consider the response of another young *doulos* to that choice. In Psalm 40, David sang his answer to God:

> My ears you have pierced . . . then I said, "Here I am, I have come . . . to do your will, O my God, is my desire; your law is within my heart."

Epilog

As I write this, I am still reflecting on a conversation I had earlier this week.

A Ukrainian friend was visiting Seattle for a few days and, now that the need for all the pre-glasnost security about Christian ministry in what used to be the Soviet Union has been coming to an end, I was giving my friend a fuller picture of the scope and purposes of the *Worldwide Student NetWork*. My friend has always known that we were Christians.

"It's not like Christians are trying to come in and change the Soviet Union," I began. Before I could continue, my friend smiled wryly and looked away. It was clear that he had noticed the barrage of Christian attention on his nation since the new openness and, like strong people everywhere, he had rejected the notion that he and his tenacious countrymen and women needed rescuing. These are the people, after all, who never stopped chafing under communism. They never really complied.

As I gazed at my friend that night, both realities were clear to me. For nearly three generations, the profound spiritual roots of his proud national heritage have been systematically choked by militant, bureaucratic atheism. In that spiritual vacuum, this strong young man has survived three years of tough military service in an Islamic country, he has endured the way-of-life inequities of an unjust society and he worries about things ever being any different for his three-year-old daughter.

The truest thing about my friend is that he is spiritually "harassed and helpless." He does not yet know the Shepherd. It is also true that when he hears the truth from me, it must continue to be with a dialog of respect and thoughtfulness. He simply needs me to bear witness, without condescension, to what I know about Christ. He needs to trust me.

The non-Christians, both here and abroad, that you and I love and have introduced to Christ have not been merely lost people who needed saving. Most of them are inquisitive, ambitious survivors who are a joy to encounter. And when they come to know Christ and become our compatriots, they are powerful people of faith.

Perhaps you will make a career of digging down deep into understanding those two realities.

Jesus Christ loves to bestow on ordinary people like you and me a life that:

- requires boldness;

- gives significance via relationships, usually along with discipline and sacrifice; and that

- charges our imagination with its scope.

At our Lord's gracious invitation, the sweeping redemptive dreams of His great heart are ours to share. And someday, men and women from every tribe and people and nation and tongue will join us in crowding around to celebrate with Him.

Lessons I Have Learned in Over Fifty Years of Helping to Establish National and Worldwide Movements

John R. Mott
Given at Rochester, New York, 1943

1. Jesus Christ constitutes the only enduring foundation for a movement with objectives like ours.

2. The vital processes should have right of way.

   What are the most vital processes?

   A. Exposing men to Christ Himself. He will then make His own impression and if He makes the impression, it will be profound, transforming and enduring.

   B. The intensive and appropriate study of the original writings of the Christian faith—Bible study.

   C. The practice and discipline of prayer and intercessory action.

   D. Augmenting the leadership of the Christian forces. "He who does the work is not so profitably employed as he who multiplies the doers." Count the day lost that you do not do something, either directly or indirectly, to multiply the number of unselfish workers.

3. It is easier to attempt and carry to success large and exacting undertakings than small ones.

   A. It is the impossible situations which bring out our own latent powers.

   B. If we do not have tasks that we honestly know are too difficult for our own wisdom and strength, we are by no means so likely to avail ourselves of our superhuman resources.

4. The heroic appeal makes possible the heroic response. The strongest men can be inspired to accomplishment by putting before them something that is really baffling and truly significant.

5. Make the gospel difficult and you make it triumphant. "Christ never hid his scars to win a disciple." The application of the principle of sacrifice invariably ensures the largest fruitage.

6. It is highly important that we study and employ strategy. This constitutes the means of doing with smaller forces that which we cannot do with large forces without strategy. One of the most strategic times to work is in time of war. Man's extremity is God's opportunity.

7. Give right of way to . . . strategic classes, for example students, men of the armed forces, rulers of nations . . . Keep in mind not only strategic classes, but also strategic places, methods and times.

8. Nothing takes the place of hard work.

9. No great work can be satisfactorily administered from an office chair. We must appear on the battlefield.

10. In any work abounding in pressing needs and great opportunities, we must make a study of priorities. We must plan the use of our time.

11. It is not necessary that we do so many things, or that we have our own way, but it is necessary that we should be Christlike.

12. We should never be content with second best.

13. Group thinking, planning, and action constitute the most highly multiplying method. Christ sent workers out two by two and in groups. We cannot know the full mind of our Lord or achieve the finest and largest results if we play a lone hand.

14. Loyalty is the cardinal virtue in Christian work. After wide observation and prolonged study of biography, I place it first. Loyalty insures unity, confidence, liberty and power in all Christian movements which year in and year out achieve the greatest spiritual results.

15. We must be constantly weaving into our organization the new generation. My work the world over and across the many years has shown me that young men can be trusted with great loads and great responsibilities. Youths have never disappointed me when I have put heavy burdens upon them.

16. We must preserve the power of growth and continue to grow. Remember the word of the Psalmist, "He shall be full of say; he shall bring forth fruit in old age."

17. We should live under the spell of immediacy. "I must work the works of Him who sent me when it is day, for the night cometh, when no man can work."

How Can We Connect?

There are lots of places to start in your worldwide student networking. Here are a few good resources.

A. For information about top international campuses in need of a *Worldwide Student NetWork* partnership, contact:

> *International University Resources*
> *1800 - 30th Street, Suite 312*
> *Boulder, CO 80301*
> *(303) 449-2555*
> *Fax (303) 449-6299*

These people can also tell you about the new computer program "C.T.'s World Tours."

B. Here are ideas and resources for crossing the five WSN Bridges:

1. PRAYER

❑ For help in beginning a prayer movement on your campus, or to receive a quarterly copy of *Frontlines* from the National Collegiate Prayer Alliance, contact a local staff member, or send your name and address to:

> *The National Collegiate Prayer Alliance*
> *6075 Roswell Road, Suite 500*
> *Atlanta, GA 30328*
> *(404) 252-9462*

❑ To receive a quarterly copy of the *Worldwide Student NetWorker*, contact a local staff member, or send your name and address to:

> *The* Worldwide Student NetWorker
> *Campus Crusade for Christ, Dept. 25-00*
> *100 Sunport Lane*

Orlando, FL 32809
(800) 444-5335

2. GIVING

Lots of options, but here are two.

❑ Talk to your partner ministry, or even a potential partner about helping to fund their campus ministry, a special project or individual staff members.

❑ Every year the *Worldwide Student NetWork* here in the U.S. helps to underwrite projects such as special international training conferences. For more information about what we're raising funds for this year, write to:

John Rogers
Worldwide Student NetWork
Campus Crusade for Christ, Dept. 25-00
100 Sunport Lane
Orlando, FL 32809
(800) 444-5335

3. GOING

❑ *International Summer Projects*

Write or call for this year's brochure:

Worldwide Student NetWork
Campus Christ for Christ, Dept. 25-50
100 Sunport Lane
Orlando, FL 32809
(800) 444-5335

❑ *STINT (Short-Term, International)*

Two semesters of ministry during the school year with an American or international team at an international partnership campus.

For an application and/or information, contact:

> *Campus STINT*
> *Campus Crusade for Christ, Dept. 25-50*
> *100 Sunport Lane*
> *Orlando, FL 32809*
> *(800) 444-5335*

❑ *Serving long-term (three to five years or more) internationally*

For more information about qualifications and locations, contact:

> *International Resource Ministries*
> *Campus Crusade for Christ, Dept. 28-00*
> *100 Sunport Lane*
> *Orlando, FL 32809*
> *(800) 444-5335*

❑ *Staff opportunities with Campus Crusade for Christ in the U.S.*

Call: (800) 444-5335

4. PERSONALIZING

❑ For resources, ideas, and a catalog of foreign language materials you can use with international students, contact:

> *International Student Resources*
> *A Ministry of Campus Crusade for Christ*
> *P.O. Box 14309*
> *Minneapolis, MN 55414*
> *(612) 379-7066*
> *Fax: (612) 379-9372*

5. MOBILIZING/SENDING

International ministries expect us to arrive having already been equipped for a personal ministry in their countries. Principles are the same in most countries, but specific materials are being tailored by each country. If you understand and can communicate the principles of building a campus ministry in your home culture, you will be able to apply those principles in your partner's culture as well.

❏ To schedule an equipping seminar, or to find out about the annual conferences at Christmas and spring break in various parts of the U.S., contact your local staff team. If you need a phone number for the team nearest you, contact:

Student LINC Ministry
Campus Crusade for Christ, Dept. 25-SL
100 Sunport Lane
Orlando, FL 32809
(800) 678-LINC

❏ For help in starting a new chapter of Campus Crusade for Christ/the *Worldwide Student NetWork*, contact:

Student LINC Ministry
Campus Crusade for Christ, Dept. 25-SL
100 Sunport Lane
Orlando, FL 32809
(800) 678-LINC

Notes

1. Clarence P. Shedd, *Two Centuries of Student Movements,* (New York: Association Press, 1934), p. 1.

2. Donald G. Shockley, *Campus Ministry: The Church Beyond Itself,* (Louisville: Westminster/John Knox Press, 1989), p. 91.

3. Ralph Winter, "Crucial Issues in Missions: Working Toward the Year 2000," *Mission Frontiers,* June-October, 1990, p. 37.

4. Shockley, *Campus Ministry,* p. 14.

5. Shockley, *Campus Ministry,* p. 106.

6. John Gration, "Conversion in Cultural Context," *International Bulletin of Missionary Research,* October, 1983, p. 157.

7. John Naisbitt and Patricia Aburdene, *Megatrends 2000,* (New York: William Morrow and Company, Inc., 1990), p. 11.

8. Alan Deutschman, "What 25-Year-Olds Want," *Fortune,* August 27, 1990, p. 43.

9. Deutschman, "What 25-Year-Olds Want," p. 44.

10. Aburdene and Naisbitt, *Megatrends 2000,* p. 298-99.

11. George Barna, *The Frog in the Kettle,* (Ventura, California: Regal Books, 1990), p. 170.

12. Barna, *The Frog in the Kettle,* p. 299.

13. Jay Gary, "The Meaning of the Year 2000," (Pasadena, California: Global Service Office, 1990), p. 1.

14. Rebecca Chaney, "Pioneers in Freedom," *Worldwide Challenge,* September/October, 1990, p. 81.

15. Chaney, "Pioneers in Freedom," p. 81.

16. *Worldwide Student NetWorker,* Spring 1990, p. 7.

17. South African terminology used by this team.

18. Malcolm Muggeridge, *Chronicles of Wasted Time, Vol. I: The Green Stick* (London: Collins Press, 1972), pp. 258, 259.

19. Dorothy Sayers, *The Whimsical Christian* (New York: Collier Books/Macmillan Publishing Company, 1987), p. 32.

20. Kenneth Wuest, "Romans in the Greek New Testament," *Word Studies in the Greek New Testament, Vol. I* (Grand Rapids, Michigan: Eerdmans Publishing Company, 1955), p. 250.

References

Books

Aburdene, Patricia and Naisbitt, John. *Ten New Directions For the 1990's: Megatrends 2000.* New York: William Morrow and Company, Inc., 1990.

Barna, George. *The Frog in the Kettle: What Christians Need to Know About Life in the Year 2000.* Ventura, California: Regal Books, 1990.

Barry, Dave. *Dave Barry's Only Travel Guide You'll Ever Need.* New York: Fawcett Columbine, 1991.

Barrett, David B. and Reapsome, James W. *Seven Hundred Plans to Evangelize the World: The Rise of a Global Evangelization Movement.* Birmingham, Alabama: New Hope, 1988.

Bright, Bill. *Come Help Change the World.* San Bernardino, California: Here's Life Publishers, 1985.

Carmichael, Amy. *The Gold Cord: The Story of a Fellowship.* Fort Washington, Pennsylvania: Christian Literature Crusade. First American edition, 1974.

Elliot, Elisabeth. *A Chance to Die: The Life and Legacy of Amy Carmichael.* Old Tappan, New Jersey: Fleming H. Revell Company, 1987.

Frost, Robert. *The Poems of Robert Frost.* New York: Random House, Inc., 1946, p. 117.

Gary, Jay E. *A Vision to Encompass the World: The Story of Student Movements and the Great Commission.* San Bernardino, California: Worldwide Student NetWork, 1987.

Hammarskjold, Dag. *Markings.* New York: Ballantine Books, 1983.

Howard, David M. *Student Power in World Missions.* Downers Grove, Illinois: InterVarsity Press, 1970; reprint ed., 1979.

Matthews, Basil. *John R. Mott, World Citizen.* New York: Harper and Bros., 1935.

Mott, John. *Addresses and Papers of John R. Mott, Vol.6,* "Lessons I Have Learned In Over Fifty Years of Helping to Establish National and World-Wide Christian Movements." New York: Association Press, 1946.

Muggeridge, Malcolm. *Chronicles of Wasted Time. Vol.I: The Green Stick.* London: Collins Press, 1972.

Roe, Earl O., ed. *Dream Big: The Henrietta Mears Story.* Ventura, California: Regal Books, 1990.

Rouse, Ruth. *The World's Student Christian Federation.* London: S.C.M. Press Ltd., 1948.

Sayers, Dorothy L. *The Whimsical Christian.* Previously published as *Christian Letters to a Post-Christian World.* Eerdmans Publishing Company, 1969; reprint ed., New York: Collier Books/Macmillan Publishing Company, 1987.

Shedd, Clarence. *Two Centuries of Student Christian Movements.* New York: Association Press, 1934.

Shockley, Donald G. *Campus Ministry: The Church Beyond Itself.* Louisville: Westminster/John Knox Press, 1989.

Stepping Out: A Guide to Short-Term Missions. Monrovia, California: Short-term Missions Advocates, Inc., 1987.

Tucker, Ruth A. *From Jerusalem to Irian Jaya.* Grand Rapids, Michigan: Academie Books/ Zondervan Publishing House, 1983.

Tucker, Ruth A. *Guardians of the Great Commission: The Story of Women in Modern Missions.* Grand Rapids, Michigan: Academie Books/Zondervan Publishing House, 1988.

Wallstrom, Timothy C. *The Creation of a Student Movement to Evangelize the World.* Pasadena, California: William Carey International University Press, 1980.

Wuest, Kenneth S. *Wuest's Word Studies in the Greek New Testament.* 4 Volumes. Grand Rapids, Michigan: Wm. B. Eerdmans Publishing Company, 1955.

g.- Noreen Walter

Periodicals and Reports

Barrett, David B. "Living in the World of AD 2000." *World Evangelization,* Lausanne Committee for World Evangelization. November/December, 1988, pp. 11-14.

Chaney, Rebecca. "Pioneers in Freedom." *Worldwide Challenge,* September/October, 1990, pp. 76-82.

Deutschman, Alan. "What 25-Year-Olds Want." *Fortune,* August 27, 1990, pp. 42-50.

Gary, Jay E. "The Meaning of the Year 2000." Pasadena, California: Global Service Office, 1990.

Gary, Jay E. "The Student Evangelism Index." San Bernardino, California: Worldwide Student NetWork, September, 1987.

Gration, John A. "Conversion in Cultural Context." *International Bulletin of Missionary Research,* October, 1983, pp. 157-62.

Gross, David M. and Scott, Sophronia. "Proceeding With Caution." *Time,* July 16, 1990, pp. 56-62.

Hesselgrave, David J. "Ten Major Trends in World Missions." *World Evangelization,* Lausanne Committee for World Evangelization. May/June, 1988, pp. 12-14.

Snyder, Howard A. "Ten Major Trends Facing the Church." *World Evangelization,* Lausanne Committee for World Evangelization. May/June 1988, pp. 5-11.

Westlake Hutcheson, Susan. "The Evangelization of the World in this Generation: John R. Mott and the Watchword of the Student Volunteer Movement," thesis presented for Master of Arts in Church History, Trinity Evangelical Divinity School, 1983.

Winter, Ralph D. "Crucial Issues in Missions: Working Toward the Year 2000." *Mission Frontiers,* June-October, 1990, pp. 36-38.

Winter, Ralph D. "Four Men, Three Eras." Pasadena, California: U.S. Center for World Mission. (Reprinted.)